Worlds
Seven Modern Poets
Edited by Geoffrey Summerfield

Books by Geoffrey Summerfield

The Later Poems of John Clare (with Eric Robinson)
Manchester University Press, 1964

John Clare: The Shepherd's Calendar (with. Eric Robinson)
Oxford University Press, 1964

Topics in English
Batsford, 1965

Selected Poetry and Prose of John Clare (with Eric Robinson)
Oxford University Press, 1966

Creativity in English
N.C.T.E., 1967

Voices
Penguin, 1968

Matthew Arnold and the Education of the New Order
(with Peter Smith)
Cambridge University Press, 1969

Essays and Addresses on Composition
Nebraska Curriculum Center, 1970

Junior Voices
Penguin, 1970

Creatures Moving
Penguin, 1970

English in Practice (with Stephen Tunnicliffe)
Cambridge University Press, 1971

The Creative Word
Random House, 1972

WORLDS
SEVEN MODERN POETS

CHARLES CAUSLEY
THOM GUNN
SEAMUS HEANEY
TED HUGHES
NORMAN MacCAIG
ADRIAN MITCHELL
EDWIN MORGAN

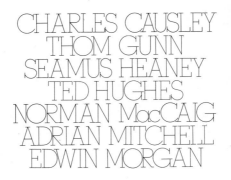
Photographs by
Fay Godwin, Larry Herman and Peter Abramowitsch

Edited by Geoffrey Summerfield
Penguin Education

Penguin Education
A Division of Penguin Books Ltd,
Harmondsworth, Middlesex, England
Penguin Books Inc, 7110 Ambassador Road,
Baltimore, Md 21207, USA
Penguin Books Australia Ltd,
Ringwood, Victoria, Australia
Penguin Books Canada Ltd,
41 Steelcase Road West,
Markham, Ontario, Canada
Penguin Books (N.Z.) Ltd,
182–190 Wairau Road, Auckland 10, New Zealand

First published 1974
This selection copyright © Geoffrey Summerfield, 1974
Introduction and notes copyright © Geoffrey Summerfield, 1974
Copyright acknowledgement for items in this volume will be found on page 279

Designed by Stuart Jackman
Made and printed in Great Britain by
Butler & Tanner Ltd, Frome and London
Set in Monophoto Photina by Oliver Burridge Filmsetting Ltd, Crawley, Sussex

My part in this is for
Jo Miles
Morton Paley
Alex and Florence Zwerdling

CONTENTS

PREFACE

Some brief words of thanks. First, and emphatically, to the poets in this book who have been unstintingly generous – almost embarrassingly so at times – with their time, cooperation, encouragement. Their kindness made the making of the book an even greater pleasure than I had anticipated. Thanks also to Martin Lightfoot of Penguin Education for his tireless interest and support, and for the invitation.

Finally, thanks to Catherine for her continuing help and co-operation.

Geoffrey Summerfield
University of York, 1973

INTRODUCTION

The seven poets in this anthology do not represent a total picture of the recent poetic scene in Britain, but rather a range of the best poetry of the recent past and of the present. It is a range that includes an extraordinary variety, and a consistently rewarding level of sheer competence and of attention to the world – and the competence and the attention are related, for (in the words of an American poet) 'craft is perfected attention'. It is primarily this variety that I have tried to reflect in choosing the poets and their poems.

Needless to say, there are omissions that will irritate, puzzle, annoy or frustrate any one reader, so some words of explanation may be in order. The audience I have in mind is not so much the mature reader returning to, and extending, familiar pleasures, nor the curious and adventurous follower of a series like *Penguin Modern Poets*. I would not exclude such readers; indeed I would welcome them. But I have been mostly preoccupied with the needs of the younger adult who wants to move more deeply into contemporary British poetry.

Anyone who bears this in mind will understand, I hope, why I have chosen, regretfully, not to include two such very good poets as Charles Tomlinson and Geoffrey Hill. Charles Tomlinson's poetry is far removed from the distinctive intensities and preoccupations of early adulthood. Geoffrey Hill's splendidly resonant and hermetic poetry yields up its satisfactions but slowly. I have been tempted to include them both because I greatly admire their work: for some things I think they are the best poets of their respective generations and their absence from this volume should not be misinterpreted. In a similar way I resisted the tempting notion of including a representative selection from the work of Ian Hamilton Finlay. In this instance I stayed my hand because I think the younger reader may well be puzzled, or even deterred, by the apparent eccentricity of Finlay's poetry – though it is capable of giving rare pleasure to experienced readers. I consulted Philip Larkin about his inclusion in this volume: Mr Larkin's view was that he would prefer not to collaborate with attempts to make his poetry more accessible to younger readers. Finally, I regret the omission of women poets from this book. This is simply due to the fact that Britain in the last fifteen years or so has not produced a woman poet of real stature. The American scene is very different, and if Denise Levertov had not emigrated to the States many moons ago she would undoubtedly be included here. As it is, this is an exclusively male volume – though if I were compiling it five years or so from now I think I would find Anne Stevenson a strong candidate.

Reading once again the poems in this selection, certain general observations suggest themselves. William Stafford has remarked that 'we talk and write the days of our lives'. One of the central facts about our lives is that they are lived *somewhere*, in a particular place. And the poems, here, speak of a variety of places, and a variety of ways of being conscious of place, of a sense of being located: both of being where you want or have to be, and of being where all is not, alas, well. In an extended sense of the word we are also 'located' in a world of ideas, anxieties, delights, discoveries and so on, both privately and publicly. If, therefore, Edwin Morgan unmistakably speaks and writes from, and of, Glasgow, he also happens to speak and write from the first decade of space-probes. Charles Causley, on the other hand, speaks from a sense of being *rooted* in Cornwall and also speaks, as it were, from the past of Cornwall, its misty days of sorrow, tragedy and magic. Thom Gunn goes West and writes of California, his adopted home, with generously appreciative delight.

Poets share, too, the language of the community into which they were born or in which they live. That language carries with it a sense of the world, an attitude towards other people, and a feeling for the precise way in which language can cope with the world, mirror it, change it, embody it. Is it a coincidence that all the poets in this book have enjoyed or now enjoy the resources of a speech which, in some way, is in conflict with 'standard English'? If it *is* a coincidence, it is not a trivial one. Consider the significances of Norman MacCaig and Edwin Morgan as English-speaking Scotsmen; Charles Causley, from and in Cornwall, with the death of a local Celtic language not so many years behind him; Ted Hughes from the West Riding of Yorkshire; Thom Gunn, now enjoying the Californian language; Adrian Mitchell, finding a voice and style in the idioms of the radical Left; and Seamus Heaney, drawing on an English heavily soaked in Irish influences.

Needless to say, the lives of the poets contain not only the same kinds of events as we all experience, but also the pressures and nudgings of the presence of other poets. This is explicitly expressed in Thom Gunn's 'My Sad Captains' where he acknowledges the beneficent presence of a 'choir invisible' of those who have actually been present in his life – parents, friends and so on – and of those who have informed his life through the word on the page: and the very title – a deft quotation from Shakespeare's *Antony and Cleopatra* – points to one of the most fruitful influences on Gunn's own poetry. In another way, the music of Charlie Parker and of Duke Ellington have been an important part of Adrian Mitchell's life. Not only does he write poetry about, and (as it were) for such men – who have given him 'gifts' – but he also writes a poetry that has itself been influenced by them, as a medium, as a tone of voice, as a rhythm.

We, the readers, have also been in our own several ways where the poets have been. Like Edwin Morgan we have perhaps been disturbed exhilaratingly by space-exploits, and like Norman MacCaig have 'fallen in love'. But just as poetry can help us to rediscover, with a refreshed vividness, the actualities and truths of our own past lives, so it can also point us forward to new forms of consciousness. Seamus Heaney can nudge us into a discovery of country matters and of the extraordinariness of the ordinary, just as Adrian Mitchell, in a different way, discovers for us new forms of fun, good humour and fine anger.

Many of us 'write poetry', especially in adolescence, and then grow older without either need or stamina to continue. In this sense we can usefully say that poets continue to live with the intensity and the need to speak out of that intensity that we found sporadically in adolescence. How, then, does a poet get started? Why does he persist? What kinds of risks, burdens does this persistence involve? Where was he when he felt compelled to speak, to speak of, to speak out?

It is to suggest some answers to such questions that some of the poets agreed to offer for this volume an account of their own ways into the making of poetry, of what fed their minds and imaginations, of what provoked and sustained them. I once asked William Stafford to consider these questions, and I'd like to quote his reply, if only for the pleasure of sharing it with you:

It is easy to say my background: born in a Kansas town, growing years in various towns, a steady family life with brother and sister, a habit of reading, and a succession of allegiances to writers like Cooper, Hudson, Scott, Cather, Hardy. But to repeat the details is to blur the main point, in my opinion: a writer is not someone to whom outwardly significant things happen, but a person whose activity for one reason or another turns toward a certain way of dealing with language and experience. That certain way is simply to be willing to start with local, insignificant ideas or phrases, and to have faith in them. Results grow from lending one's attention to the daily language and to the inner experience one is having. We all live in a torrent of mental and verbal events; in that torrent writers sift out and combine elements that interest them.

No special sensitivity or intelligence is required – though for other activities, sensitivity and intelligence would be good to have. The crucial thing is just willing involvement with the nuances and suggestions that thrive in language and thought. Influences that make the most difference are close and sustained. For myself, I have not been able to dredge up a literary voice that influenced me so much as my mother's voice did. I must witness for the influences of immediate, ordinary interaction. We talk and write the days of our lives, and it is willingness to start from where we are that enables us to have a good life locally and make 'original' things – art.

It has been dustily suggested that a book such as this is 'more appropriate to the dead than the living'. I happen to believe that there is an urgent sense in which we need to understand the living, those who speak and write of our own times and places. They can, I suggest, amplify, refine, enrich and sharpen the ways in which we come to perceive and speak of our own living. It is in this way that poetry is, in the useful word of Marianne Moore, 'useful'. And I hope that, more modestly, the way in which this particular collection is organized will also prove 'useful'.

Throughout this book passages in **bold type** are the words of the poets themselves, either specially written for this book or culled from various published sources. The photographs aim either to show the poets in their various worlds or to offer representations of local facts, particular places, particular people which at some time or other have provided these poets with pleasure or significant memory. They are not 'illustrations', but a reminder that poems, like poets, come out of the world we know, and that that is where they belong.

CHARLES CAUSLEY

PHOTOGRAPHS BY
FAY GODWIN

Charles Causley was born in Launceston, Cornwall, in 1917, where he still writes and teaches. I think I became a working poet the day I joined the destroyer Eclipse at Scapa Flow in August, 1940. I came out of the Navy in 1946 and became a teacher. In the thirties I worked for a builder, and also in the office of an electricity corporation. I also played the piano in a small four-piece dance band for years in the 1930s. . . . I wrote only fragmentary notes and sketches until 1943, but I can date my first poem in May of that year.

His publications include: *Farewell, Aggie Weston* (1951), *Survivor's Leave* (1953), *Union Street* (1957), *Johnny Alleluia* (1961), *Underneath the Water* (1968), *Figgie Hobbin* (1970) and two anthologies: *Rising Early* and *Dawn to Dusk*.

I was born in Launceston, a little market-town in north Cornwall, and went to the local National School: a huge, booming, granite-and-slate building stranded like a stone ark on the edge of the borough allotments. It had been put up in 1840, and looked it: the name and date over the front door had begun to crumble long before I first attended there in the 1920s. I went to three schools, but this was the one where I was happiest: possibly because most of the time I was there I was in a state of innocence. Lost innocence, of one form and another, is a strong thread in the work of many poets. I am not talking here merely about loss of virtue. I mean that in those days the world still seemed to me just made, Eden-fresh. Nothing had happened yet to change my scale of values.

Up to about the age of eleven, I don't remember hearing much poetry at all. We must have had some at school, because a few lines have stuck in my mind, like waste matter that refuses to be disposed of down a drain. For instance, there was this by Sir Walter Scott.

O, young Lochinvar is come out of the west,
Through all the wide Border his steed was the best.

Who young Lochinvar was, and why he had come out of the west, have remained hazy in my memory. But, undeniably, he is still there. Then there were some lines by Tennyson.

The splendour falls on castle walls
And snowy summits old in story.

Could those walls have been the slowly disintegrating lumps of Norman castle we could see through the high windows of the classroom? Probably not; poetry was about something that went on somewhere else, far away. I had a vague idea, though, that another piece by Tennyson may have been set a bit nearer home.

So all day long the noise of battle roll'd
Among the mountains by the winter sea.

Didn't King Arthur fight his last battle in Cornwall, and wasn't his sword Excalibur finally thrown into the mysterious waters of Dozmary Pool, high on Bodmin Moor? That was only a dozen miles away, but I'd never been there. Nobody in our family had a car, and most people remained pretty solidly in one place in Cornwall in those days. Anyhow, if we did go away it was to the real seaside, with sand on the beach: to Trebarwith and Bude, by train, or to Polzeath by charabanc on the annual Sunday School outing.

The sea made a profound impression on me. I sensed it instantly as a sulky, dangerous, beautiful, unpredictable element. Just as it was pretending to be at its friendliest, it could drag you under and kill you.

I knew hardly any poetry, but I read a lot of prose: anything, everything. One of my favourite books was an abridged version of David Copperfield. I never forgot the passage where Little Em'ly, on the beach at Yarmouth, says – after David has declared boldly that he isn't afraid of the sea – 'Ah! but it's cruel. I have seen it tear a boat as big as our house all to pieces.'

I can see myself now, reading those lines, cold with terror, as I lay on my stomach on the kitchen floor of our slate-fronted house at 18, St Thomas Hill; and the remembrance of reading it as a child came back to me again and again in 1940, when I found myself, scared stiff, bouncing about in a destroyer in the Atlantic.

I was glad Launceston was an inland town. The thought of the sea knocking continuously almost at the door of one's house filled me with a profound unease. Yet it had a terrible fascination. My mother used to take me to the tiny church of St Thomas the Apostle, where I had been baptized. Often, on Sunday evenings, we'd sing Baring-Gould's famous hymn 'Now the day is over'. I was born at Riverside, a hundred yards from the church, with a river – it had a particularly high, liquid note – rattling past, and a fast little stream running into it just under our kitchen window. No wonder I seem always to have been haunted by the sound of water. When, in church, we got to

Grant to little children
    Visions bright of Thee;
Guard the sailors tossing
    On the deep blue sea

the building always appeared to me to give a lurch, as though we were really on a ship. The contents of Hymns Ancient and Modern printed themselves on my mind; and so did the songs I heard sung by the ex-soldiers who had survived the First World War. My father had been a private soldier in France. I only remember him as a sick man; he had been invalided out of the Army, and died in 1924. What had really happened in France? Nobody ever told me directly; but my first clues came from the songs.

If you want to find the old battalion,
I know where they are, I know where they are,
    I know where they are. . . .
They're hanging on the old barbed wire.
I've seen 'em, I've seen 'em,
Hanging on the old barbed wire. . . .

And there was a terrifying version of 'If you were the only girl in the world':

If you were the only Boche in the trench
And I had the only bomb,
Nothing else would matter in the world that day,
I would blow you up into eternity.
Chamber of Horrors, just made for two,
With nothing to spoil our fun;
There would be such a heap of things to do,
I should get your rifle and bayonet too. . . .

After this, most of the poetry we read at the grammar school seemed pretty thin stuff. It's true, though, that the world, the time-scale, of poetry had moved a shade nearer that Young Lochinvar and King Arthur. Now it all seemed to be cricket, bull-dogs, drinking ale in Sussex pubs, cuckoos and a rather picture-postcard view of the countryside that was somehow at variance with the realities of rural life and work around me. We also read some Shakespeare. I couldn't follow it very well, but liked the sound.

It never occurred to me to write a poem at school unless I was asked to by a teacher. To my surprise, writing verse didn't appear too difficult. Even better, for the first time, something I'd done was treated with grave approval, even admiration, by my schoolmates. This was when my first poem, written when I was thirteen, got ten marks out of ten from my hero the English master, B. F. Hobby, a football- and rugby-playing Welshman who also taught French and History, and who was reputed never to give full marks for anything. My poem was a sonnet called 'The Jew'.

Beneath yon towering palm-tree's lengthening shade,
Now as the brazen evening sun doth fade
A veritable Shylock of all Jews
Doth count his gold for fear that he might lose
One dinar of his hoarded, glittering pile,
While by him flows the muddy, sluggish Nile. . . .

I still feel guilty about bringing in the Nile, but at the time I couldn't fit in anything else to rhyme with pile. B. F. Hobby demurred a bit at the word 'veritable', but apart from this he was enthusiastic, and for the first and last time in my school life my stock rose.

I was always hypnotized by the sound of words. My early childhood was over before we had a radio, and I was apt to use words without knowing how to pronounce them. Later on, carefully-spoken radio announcers helped to improve things for me. The next poem I wrote was on the subject of Robespierre. At least I wasn't being unconsciously anti-Semitic this time: but I still seem to have had a mania for writing about people and situations I knew nothing about. (During the whole of my school career, I never got beyond 1714 in history.) When I wrote the poem, I must have been working my way through Baroness Orczy's novels about the Scarlet Pimpernel. The poem began:

O Robespierre, thou sea-green immobile,
Thy soul, deep-stained, was ice and did not feel. . . .

I forget what it didn't feel. Obviously, I had no idea what 'immobile' meant, and it never occurred to me to look it up in a dictionary. Anyway, I pronounced it 'immobeel'. B. F. Hobby was a little cooler about this one. 'Ha!' he said. 'I see where you get that from. It was Carlyle who called Robespierre "the seagreen incorruptible".' At the time, I thought Carlyle was a town in Scotland, but I didn't let on. Eight out of ten.

My first job was as a clerk in the office (a sort of greenhouse attached to a private house) of a building company. To me, the work was stupefyingly boring: though with the enormous unemployment figures of the early thirties, I felt I was lucky to get a job at all. But I felt I was trapped for life. Reading, and swimming, became my escape. This was in 1933, the year of the rise of Hitler. We happened to take the News Chronicle, a daily paper with a strong radical tradition and one that charted grimly the drift to a war that it seemed would inevitably engulf me and my contemporaries. I read books by George Orwell, Arthur Koestler, Christopher Isherwood; and through the pages of the New Statesman I became familiar with the poetry of W. H. Auden, Louis MacNeice, Stephen Spender, Cecil Day Lewis, and I discovered the work of older poets like T. S. Eliot and Ezra Pound.

Brilliantly-edited collections of poetry and prose began to appear, like John Lehmann's New Writing and Daylight and (later) Horizon, a magazine edited by Cyril Connolly and Spender. The poetry and prose in them dealt, as often as not, with the here and now. None of the writers pretended that the war wasn't likely to happen. They communicated a marvellous sense of imaginative reality, and helped to alleviate the oppression of spending one's teens under the long shadows of Hitler, Mussolini, Franco and the Spanish Civil War. By this time, too, I had read most of the writers of the First World War: Robert Graves, Wilfred Owen, Edmund Blunden, Edward Thomas, Siegfried Sassoon. On my first holiday in London, I bought a second-hand copy of Siegfried Sassoon's war poems in a second-hand book-shop in the Charing Cross Road. His were the first poems I learnt by heart because I wanted to carry them round with me all the time, wherever I was.

'Good-morning; good-morning!' the General said
When we met him last week on our way to the Line,
Now the soldiers he smiled at are most of 'em dead,
And we're cursing his staff for incompetent swine.

The words: clear, hard as stones, spoke clearly and seemed to crystallize my confused feelings about poetry; to point a way. All through the thirties I had been trying to write. But everything I knew anything about seemed parochial, trivial, written about before. Then there was the difficulty of choosing a form: the play or novel or story or poem. Which should I stick at? It was Hitler who decided that for me.

In 1940 I was called up, and for the first time was wrenched irretrievably from my home-environment. There was no question of packing my bag and deciding to come home again after a day or two, as in 'Reservoir Street'. I found myself thrown on my own resources. I didn't know how to cook, sew, scrub a deck, wash and iron clothes, for instance: all essential if one is to survive on the lower-deck.

I was acutely home- as well as sea-sick. The sea had lost none of its terrors for me. Among the pleasures, on the other hand, were the exotica of travel. I never missed the opportunity of stepping ashore, however unpromising the prospect, on journeys from Scapa Flow to Sydney, and from Freetown in West Africa to New Guinea. From the moment I joined my first ship, I was spellbound by the sailors' lingo: about 500 basic words, about 495 of which I had never heard before. It was as full of poetry as the speech of Shakespeare's England: 'grab-hooks' for fingers, 'stagger juice' for rum, 'stroppy' for argumentative, 'oppoe' for friend, 'tin fish' for torpedo, 'in the rattle' for being in trouble with authority, and all the rest.

I wrote nothing for the first years of the war, but crammed the experiences in my head like a seaman stowing stray gear into a scranbag. Time, I felt, would sort it all out; the immediate objective was to survive. The Navy certainly gave me my first subjects: separation, loss, death in alien places, extraordinary characters, a perpetual sense of unease about how things might end. (It didn't give me my theme: I take this to be constant, and to represent a writer's whole attitude to life.)

The routine of living and working on the lower-deck meant that any sustained writing in prose was impossible. What I found I could do was to brood almost endlessly on a subject, teasing and worrying it out in my mind as I worked on routine jobs. The result could be scribbled down on odd bits of paper. I've often thought that (unlike the playwright, the novelist, the short-story writer) the poet's sole advantage is that with a little ingenuity he can work anywhere, at any time: on top of a bus, in a bar, in the middle of a crowd, even when apparently engaged in conversation with other people.

The unfamiliar Naval life gave me confidence to write of a world that most of my contemporaries knew little about. Returning to Cornwall after the war, I saw its sights, heard its sounds and echoes, its forms of speech, as though I had been newly born. Nowadays, I know that a poet, in order to write, doesn't have necessarily to go anywhere or do anything. The poetry is under one's nose, waiting to be gathered. Nobody told me that. If they had, before 1940, I doubt if I would have believed them.

I'm very concerned about communicating with a reader – no use talking on a dead line. But a poem mustn't be allowed to burn itself out in one brilliant flash; the poem mustn't be so explicit that there's no reason for the reader's imagination and sensibility to get working. The poet just has to decide where and when he stops simplifying the thing and allows the reader to take over. I don't know why I write ballads (the number I've written isn't all that high), only that the theme chooses the form and not the other way round. I've always enjoyed telling stories, singing and listening to music; obviously I couldn't keep these factors out of my work even if I wanted to. In any case, every poem – whatever the form – is an 'entertainment' in the best sense of the word, and tells a story. I think it's important to remember that a simple statement (and it's a lot easier to make a complicated one) isn't necessarily shallow or superficial. I don't think readers need strain their eyes at reading between the lines: more important to look at the words on the lines. A poet usually says what he means and chooses his words with much greater care than a lot of people imagine. They are as important a choice as, say, selecting one's own individual teeth.

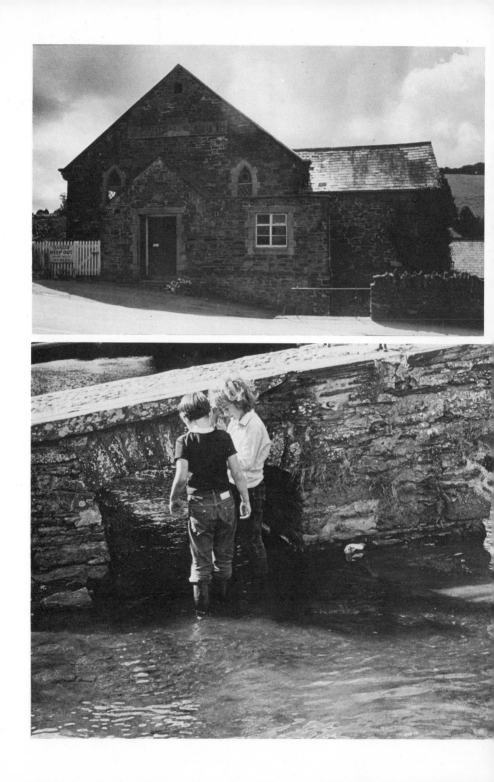

By St Thomas Water

By St Thomas Water
Where the river is thin
We looked for a jam-jar
To catch the quick fish in.
Through St Thomas Church-yard
Jessie and I ran
The day we took the jam-pot
Off the dead man.

On the scuffed tombstone
The grey flowers fell,
Cracked was the water,
Silent the shell.
The snake for an emblem
Swirled on the slab,
Across the beach of sky the sun
Crawled like a crab.

'If we walk,' said Jessie,
'Seven times round,
We shall hear a dead man
Speaking underground.'
Round the stone we danced, we sang,
Watched the sun drop,
Laid our heads and listened
At the tomb-top.

Soft as the thunder
At the storm's start
I heard a voice as clear as blood,
Strong as the heart.
But what words were spoken
I can never say,
I shut my fingers round my head,
Drove them away.

'What are those letters, Jessie,
Cut so sharp and trim
All round this holy stone
With earth up to the brim?'
Jessie traced the letters
Black as coffin-lead.
'He is not dead but sleeping,'
Slowly she said.

I looked at Jessie,
Jessie looked at me,
And our eyes in wonder
Grew wide as the sea.
Past the green and bending stones
We fled hand in hand,
Silent through the tongues of grass
To the river strand.

By the creaking cypress
We moved as soft as smoke
For fear all the people
Underneath awoke.
Over all the sleepers
We darted light as snow
In case they opened up their eyes,
Called us from below.

Many a day has faltered
Into many a year
Since the dead awoke and spoke
And we would not hear.
Waiting in the cold grass
Under a crinkled bough,
Quiet stone, cautious stone,
What do you tell me now?

Reservoir Street

In nineteen twenty-six, the year
Of the Strike, on a day of bubbling heat
I went to stay with my sun-faced cousins
Who lived in a house on Reservoir Street.

Auntie stood strong as the Eddystone Lighthouse.
A terrible light shone out of her head.
Her children scuttled like ships for harbour.
You must let them know what's what, she said.

Her five prime-beef boys circled round me.
They didn't enjoy what they saw at all.
We couldn't make any more of each other
Than the map of stains on the bedroom wall.

All night long on the road to the city
The motor-car tyres rubbed out the dark.
Early in the morning I watched from the window
The sun like a killer come out of the park.

Down in the reservoir I saw a man drowning.
His flooding head came over the side.
They poked him out of a parcel of water.
He's poisoned the drink! my cousins cried.

I packed my bag and I said to Auntie,
I think I'll go home on the one o'clock train.
My, they all said, he wants his mammy.
They never let me forget it again.

Through the Cornish jungle-country
Like a parrot the train screamed home.
I thought of my brother who slept beside me,
Four walls round us pure as cloam.

When I got to the house my head was thunder.
The bed lay open as a shell.
Sweet was my brother's kiss, and sweeter
The innocent water from the well.

Dockacre

Two doors away, at Dockacre, a ghost
In an isosceles cap assembles just before dawn,
Jerks round the ripped garden, through the dog-gates
And up the buckled stairs, quietly playing a flute.

Often, sleepless in a bland electric glare
(Since I slept on the mess-deck, to wake up
Without a pilot-light gives me the feeling
I'm going to be drowned) I've tried to hear it

Rounding the hollyhocks for the front door, but so far
It's always been the paper-train. The ghost's name
Is Nicholas Herle, once High Sheriff of Cornwall.
On the wall at Dockacre there's a creamy portrait of the
    wife

Who was shot by accident, stabbed, or driven mad,
No-one seems quite certain which, though probably
It was the last. In a curled account
He shut the girl in a dark room, trying

To starve her to sanity. She died of the cure
On Christmas Day, 1714, and Nicholas left for Hampstead,
But we've never forgotten her, or him.
My neighbour still has the bald flute. It's part

Of a cane walking-stick. He kindly offered
To play it to me once, but I declined,
Fearing that I might hear it again in the chopped hours:
Nicholas playing his inaccurate, sad tunes

As I whistled mine; both of us suffering from the same
Malaise that evidently even death won't cure.
I feared that as I looked towards my bedroom door
I should see the handle break slowly into flames, then turn.

Death of a Poet

Suddenly his mouth filled with sand.
His tractor of blood stopped thumping.
He held five icicles in each hand.
His heart packed up jumping.

His face turned the colour of something forgotten in the
    larder.
His thirty-two teeth were expelled on the kitchen floor.
His muscles, at long last, got considerably harder.
He felt younger than he had for some time before.

Four heroes, steady as wrestlers, each carried him on a
    shoulder
Into a great grey church laid out like a brain.
An iron bowl sent out stiff rays of chrysanthemums. It
    grew colder.
The sun, as expected, failed to break through the pane.

The parson boomed like a dockyard gun at a christening.
Somebody read from the bible. It seemed hours.
I got the feeling you were curled up inside the box,
    listening.
There was the thud of hymn-books, the stench of flowers.

I remembered hearing your voice on a bloody foment
Of Atlantic waters. The words burned clear as a flare.
Life begins, you said, as of this moment.
A bird flew down out of the hurling air.

Over the church a bell broke like a wave upended.
The hearse left for winter with a lingering hiss.
I looked in the wet sky for a sign, but no bird descended.
I went across the road to the pub; wrote this.

The Question

In the locked sky beats a dove.
It speaks continually of love.

Deep in the river a talking stone
Says he lies easy who lies alone.

Under the stone there hides a knife:
The beginning and end of every life.

In the dark forest are flowers of light
That never fade by day or night.

Down in the valley stands a tree,
Its roots uneasy as the sea.

High on the tree there hangs a nest.
Here, says the wind, you must take your rest.

Through the spinney with eyes of wax
Runs the woodman with glaring axe.

Naked, my love and I arise
Bathed in his fearful prophecies.

Whose is the bird and whose the stone,
Whose is the light on the midnight sown?

Whose is the tree and whose the rest,
And whose is the knife upon my breast?

Who is the woodman and what does he cry?
Gaze in the mirror. Do not reply.

In Coventry

In Coventry, that ruddled city,
Under a metal, shunting sky,
I sat in the cracked cathedral,
The holiday-makers limping by.

Christ hung down like a hawk-moth caterpillar,
Down his cheeks ran woollen tears.
On the chapel gate his crown of thorns
Was made by the Royal Engineers.

As I walked through the glittering Precinct
All the retablos burned like gold.
I heard a gear-change of bones behind me.
I saw a man lying, flat-out, cold.

He hit the slabs as though he'd been sand-bagged.
A thicket of blood sprang on his face.
We looked for a seat to lay him out on,
But man must keep moving in that place.

The rain fell down the concrete mountain.
Four friends came back, breathing hard.
Pull yourself together, Taff, they chunnered.
But his legs were butter and his face was lard.

Taff, don't let us down, they were saying.
Taff looked dead and half-buried already,
As on a river of whisky he'd taken
The quickest way out of Coventry city.

Later, on a weir of steps, I saw him
Stumbling, alone; past hopes and fears.
The blood and hair on his jagged brow
Held in place by the engineers.

Immunity

Lining up with the naked sailors,
The smell of Africa blown off-shore,
I watched the sweat run down to my ankles,
Borrowed a tickler from the man next door.

The sick-bay tiffy looked more like a doctor.
The quack was nervous, his face of bread;
He might have been last man in for England,
The sky gone dark and the pitch turned red.

It's nothing, he said as he dipped the needle,
Pumped it full of jungle juice.
Don't look at the man in front, that's the secret.
It's not like putting your head through a noose.

We stuck out our arms. He looked at his needle,
Showed the usual pusser's restraint,
Suddenly swallowed his oath to Hippocrates,
Fell on the deck in a number-one faint.

No one issued with a jab at Freetown.
No one complained of feeling crook.
Malaria, yellow and blackwater fever
Lay down low till we pulled up the hook.

Rocked on the antiseptic ocean
Nobody noticed the turning screw.
This would cost a fortune, we said, in peace-time,
The sun so yellow and the sea so blue.

And, for the record, off Kos a month later
Where Hippocrates lived out his term,
Most of them died of wounds or sea-water,
Including the doctor. None of a germ.

At the Grave of John Clare

Walking in the scythed churchyard, around the locked
    church,
Walking among the oaks and snails and mossed inscriptions
At first we failed to find the grave.
But a girl said: 'There he is: there is John Clare.'
And we stood, silent, by the ridged stone,
A stone of grey cheese.
There were no flowers for the dead ploughman
As the gilt clock fired off the hour,
Only the words:
A poet is born not made.

The dove-grey village lay in the Dutch landscape:
The level-crossing and the fields of wet barley,
The almshouses, the school, the Ebenezer Chapel,
The two pubs, and the signposts
To Stamford, To Maxey
From the pages of biography.
And later, sitting in the church
Among the unstuffed hassocks,
And smoking a pipe on the gate
At Maxey Crossing,
I thought of the dead poet:

Of the books and letters in the Peterborough Museum,
The huge, mad writing.
Of the way he walked, with one foot in the furrow,
Or hurried, terrified, as a child to fetch the milk from Maxey
Expecting from every turn a Caliban.
Of London, Charles Lamb and Hazlitt,
The bad grammar, the spelling, the invented words,
And the poetry bursting like a diamond bomb.
I thought of the last days, the old man
Sitting alone in the porch of All Saints' in Northampton,
And the dead poet trundling home to Helpston.

O Clare! Your poetry clear, translucent
As your lovely name,
I salute you with tears.
And, coming out on the green from *The Parting Pot*,
I notice a bicycle-tyre
Hanging from the high stone feathers of your monument.

Ou Phrontis
(to E. M. Forster)

The bells assault the maiden air,
The coachman waits with a carriage and pair,
But the bridegroom says *I won't be there,*
    I don't care!

Three times three times the banns declare
That the boys may blush and the girls may glare,
But the bridegroom is occupied elsewhere,
    I don't care!

Lord, but the neighbours all will stare,
Their temperatures jump as high as a hare,
But the bridegroom says *I've paid my fare,*
    I don't care!

The bride she waits by the bed so bare,
Soft as a pillow is her hair,
But the bridegroom jigs with the leg of a chair,
    I don't care!

Say, but her father's a millionaire,
A girdle of gold all night will she wear,
You must your foolish ways forswear.
    I don't care!

Her mother will offer, if she dare,
A ring that is rich but not so rare
If you'll keep your friendship in repair.
    I don't care!

Her sisters will give you a plum and a pear
And a diamond saddle for your mare.
O bridegroom! For the night prepare!
    I don't care!

Her seven brothers all debonair
Will do your wishes and some to spare
If from your fancy you'll forbear.
    I don't care!

Say, but a maid you wouldn't scare
Now that you've got her in your snare?
And what about your son and heir?
    I don't care!

She'll leap, she'll leap from the highest stair,
She'll drown herself in the river there,
With a silver knife her flesh she'll tear.
    I don't care!

Then another will lie in the silken lair
And cover with kisses her springing hair.
Another the bridal bed will share.
    I don't care!

I shall stand on my head on the table bare,
I shall kick my lily-white legs in the air,
I shall wash my hands of the whole affair,
    I don't care!

I Am the Great Sun
(from a Norman crucifix of 1632)

I am the great sun, but you do not see me,
   I am your husband, but you turn away.
I am the captive, but you do not free me,
   I am the captain you will not obey.

I am the truth, but you will not believe me,
   I am the city where you will not stay,
I am your wife, your child, but you will leave me,
   I am that God to whom you will not pray.

I am your counsel, but you do not hear me,
   I am the lover whom you will betray,
I am the victor, but you do not cheer me,
   I am the holy dove whom you will slay.

   I am your life, but if you will not name me,
   Seal up your soul with tears, and never blame me.

Recruiting Drive

Under the willow the willow
    I heard the butcher-bird sing,
Come out you fine young fellow
    From under your mother's wing.
I'll show you the magic garden
    That hangs in the beamy air,
The way of the lynx and the angry Sphinx
    And the fun of the freezing fair.

Lie down lie down with my daughter
    Beneath the Arabian tree,
Gaze on your face in the water
    Forget the scribbling sea.
Your pillow the nine bright shiners
    Your bed the spilling sand,
But the terrible toy of my lily-white boy
    Is the gun in his innocent hand.

You must take off your clothes for the doctor
    And stand as straight as a pin,
His hand of stone on your white breast-bone
    Where the bullets all go in.
They'll dress you in lawn and linen
    And fill you with Plymouth gin,
O the devil may wear a rose in his hair
    I'll wear my fine doe-skin.

My mother weeps as I leave her
    But I tell her it won't be long,
The murderers wail in Wandsworth Gaol
    But I shoot a more popular song.
Down in the enemy country
    Under the enemy tree
There lies a lad whose heart has gone bad
    Waiting for me, for me.

He says I have no culture
    And that when I've stormed the pass
I shall fall on the farm with a smoking arm
    And ravish his bonny lass.
Under the willow the willow
    Death spreads her dripping wings
And caught in the snare of the bleeding air
    The butcher-bird sings, sings, sings.

Helpston

Hills sank like green fleets on the land's long rim
About the village of toast-coloured stone.
Leaving the car beside *The Blue Bell*, we
Walked with a clutch of flowers the clear lane
Towards the grave.

It was well-combed, and quiet as before.
An upturned stone boat
Beached at God's thick door.
Only the water in the spiked grave-pot
Smelt sourly of death.
Yet no wind seemed to blow
From off the fen or sea
The flowers flickered in the painted pot
Like green antennae,
As though John Clare from a sounding skull
Brim with a hundred years of dirt and stone
Signalled to us;
And light suddenly breathed
Over the plain.

Later, drinking whisky in *The Bull* at Peterborough,
The face of the poet
Lying out on the rigid plain
Stared at me
As clearly as it once stared through
The glass coffin-lid
In the church-side pub on his burial day:
Head visible, to prove
The bulging brain was not taken away
By surgeons, digging through the bone and hair
As if to find poems still
Beating there;
Then, like an anchor, to be lowered fast
Out of creation's pain, the stropping wind,
Deep out of sight, into the world's mind.

I Saw a Shot-Down Angel

I saw a shot-down angel in the park
His marble blood sluicing the dyke of death,
A sailing tree firing its brown sea-mark
Where he now wintered for his wounded breath.

I heard the bird-noise of his splintered wings
Sawing the steep sierra of the sky,
On his fixed brow the jewel of the Kings
Reeked the red morning with a starving eye.

I stretched my hand to hold him from the heat,
I fetched a cloth to bind him where he bled,
I brought a bowl to wash his golden feet,
I shone my shield to save him from the dead.

My angel spat my solace in my face
And fired my fingers with his burning shawl,
Crawling in blood and silver to a place
Where he could turn his torture to the wall.

Alone I wandered in the sneaking snow
The signature of murder on my day,
And from the gallows-tree, a careful crow
Hitched its appalling wings and flew away.

At the British War Cemetery, Bayeux

I walked where in their talking graves
And shirts of earth five thousand lay,
When history with ten feasts of fire
Had eaten the red air away.

I am Christ's boy, I cried, I bear
In iron hands the bread, the fishes.
I hang with honey and with rose
This tidy wreck of all your wishes.

On your geometry of sleep
The chestnut and the fir-tree fly,
And lavender and marguerite
Forge with their flowers an English sky.

Turn now towards the belling town
Your jigsaws of impossible bone,
And rising read your rank of snow
Accurate as death upon the stone.

About your easy heads my prayers
I said with syllables of clay.
What gift, I asked, shall I bring now
Before I weep and walk away?

Take, they replied, the oak and laurel.
Take our fortune of tears and live
Like a spendthrift lover. All we ask
Is the one gift you cannot give.

Hymn for the Birth of a Royal Prince

Prince, for your throat of ice
The tigers of the sun
Rehearse with quarrels of fire
Their chosen one.

Upon your breast of lambs
The lean assassin lies
With love upon his lips
And chaos in his eyes.

About your brittle bed
The seven sharp angels stay
That from the frigid knife
You know will turn away.

The bawling organ breaks
Upon the appalling stone
Whose quiet courtier takes
Your kingdom for his own.

The warriors drub their wands,
With pearl your footsteps pave,
But dribbles at your feet
The idiot grave.

Prince, to your throne of birds
May all my passions fly
That, guilty, I may live
And you may die!

Song of the Dying Gunner A.A.1

Oh mother my mouth is full of stars
As cartridges in the tray
My blood is a twin-branched scarlet tree
And it runs all runs away.

Oh *Cooks to the Galley* is sounded off
And the lads are down in the mess
But I lie done by the forrard gun
With a bullet in my breast.

Don't send me a parcel at Christmas time
Of socks and nutty and wine
And don't depend on a long weekend
By the Great Western Railway line.

Farewell, Aggie Weston, the Barracks at Guz,
Hang my tiddley suit on the door
I'm sewn up neat in a canvas sheet
And I shan't be home no more.

HMS *Glory*

Death of an Aircraft
An incident of the Cretan campaign, 1941
(to George Psychoundakis)

One day on our village in the month of July
An aeroplane sank from the sea of the sky,
    White as a whale it smashed on the shore
    Bleeding oil and petrol all over the floor.

The Germans advanced in the vertical heat
To save the dead plane from the people of Crete,
    And round the glass wreck in a circus of snow
    Set seven mechanical sentries to go.

Seven stalking spiders about the sharp sun
Clicking like clockwork and each with a gun,
    But at *Come to the Cookhouse* they wheeled about
    And sat down to sausages and sauerkraut.

Down from the mountain burning so brown
Wriggled three heroes from Kastelo town,
    Deep in the sand they silently sank
    And each struck a match for a petrol-tank.

Up went the plane in a feather of fire
As the bubbling boys began to retire
    And, grey in the guardhouse, seven Berliners
    Lost their stripes as well as their dinners.

Down in the village, at murder-stations,
The Germans fell in friends and relations:
    But not a Kastelian snapped an eye
    As he spat in the air and prepared to die.

Not a Kastelian whispered a word
Dressed with the dust to be massacred,
    And squinted up at the sky with a frown
    As three bubbly boys came walking down.

One was sent to the county gaol
Too young for bullets if not for bail,
    But the other two were in prime condition
    To take on a load of ammunition.

In Archontiki they stood in the weather
Naked, hungry, chained together:
    Stark as the stones in the market-place,
    Under the eyes of the populace.

Their irons unlocked as their naked hearts
They faced the squad and their funeral-carts.
   The Captain cried, 'Before you're away
   Is there any last word you'd like to say?'

'I want no words,' said one, 'with my lead,
Only some water to cool my head.'
   'Water,' the other said, ''s all very fine
   But I'll be taking a glass of wine.

A glass of wine for the afternoon
With permission to sing a signature-tune!'
   And he ran the *raki* down his throat
   And took a deep breath for the leading note.

But before the squad could shoot or say
Like the impala he leapt away
   Over the rifles, under the biers,
   The bullets rattling round his ears.

'Run!' they cried to the boy of stone
Who now stood there in the street alone,
   But, 'Rather than bring revenge on your head
   It is better for me to die,' he said.

The soldiers turned their machine-guns round
And shot him down with a dreadful sound
   Scrubbed his face with perpetual dark
   And rubbed it out like a pencil mark.

But his comrade slept in the olive tree
And sailed by night on the gnawing sea,
   The soldier's silver shilling earned
   And, armed like an archangel, returned.

Mary, Mary Magdalene

On the east wall of the church of St Mary Magdalene at Launceston in Cornwall is a granite figure of the saint. The children of the town say that a stone lodged on her back will bring good luck.

Mary, Mary Magdalene
Lying on the wall,
I throw a pebble on your back.
Will it lie or fall?

Send me down for Christmas
Some stockings and some hose,
And send before the winter's end
A brand-new suit of clothes.

Mary, Mary Magdalene
Under a stony tree,
I throw a pebble on your back.
What will you send me?

*I'll send you for your Christening
A woollen robe to wear,
A shiny cup from which to sup,
And a name to bear.*

Mary, Mary Magdalene
Lying cool as snow,
What will you be sending me
When to school I go?

*I'll send a pencil and a pen
That write both clean and neat.
And I'll send to the schoolmaster
A tongue that's kind and sweet.*

Mary, Mary Magdalene
Lying in the sun,
What will you be sending me
Now I'm twenty-one?

*I'll send you down a locket
As silver as your skin,
And I'll send you a lover
To fit a gold key in.*

Mary, Mary Magdalene
Underneath the spray,
What will you be sending me
On my wedding-day?

I'll send you down some blossom,
Some ribbons and some lace,
And for the bride a veil to hide
The blushes on her face.

Mary, Mary Magdalene
Whiter than the swan,
Tell me what you'll send me,
Now my good man's dead and gone.

I'll send to you a single bed
On which you must lie,
And pillows bright where tears may light
That fall from your eye.

Mary, Mary Magdalene
Now nine months are done,
What will you be sending me
For my little son?

I'll send you for your baby
A lucky stone, and small,
To throw to Mary Magdalene
Lying on the wall.

Chief Petty Officer

He is older than the naval side of British history,
And sits
More permanent than the spider in the enormous wall.
His barefoot, coal-burning soul,
Expands, puffs like a toad, in the convict air
Of the Royal Naval Barracks at Devonport.

Here, in depôt, is his stone Nirvana:
More real than the opium-pipes,
The uninteresting relics of Edwardian foreign-commission.
And, from his thick stone box,
He surveys with a prehistoric eye the hostilities-only ratings.

He has the face of the dinosaur
That sometimes stares from old Victorian naval photographs:
That of some elderly lieutenant
With boots and a celluloid Crippen-collar,
Brass buttons and cruel ambitious eyes of almond.

He was probably made a Freemason in Hong Kong.
He has a son (on War Work) in the Dockyard,
And an appalling daughter
In the W.R.N.S.
He writes on your draft-chit,
Tobacco-permit or request-form
In a huge antique Borstal hand,
And pins notices on the board in the Chiefs' Mess
Requesting his messmates not to
Lay on the billiard table.
He is an anti-Semite, and has somewhat reactionary views,
And reads the pictures in the daily news.

And when you return from the nervous Pacific
Where the seas
Shift like sheets of plate-glass in the dazzling morning;
Or when you return
Browner than Alexander, from Malta,
Where you have leaned over the side, in harbour,
And seen in the clear water
The salmon-tins, wrecks and tiny explosions of crystal fish,
A whole war later
He will be sitting under a pusser's clock
Waiting for tot-time,
His narrow forehead ruffled by the Jutland wind.

Green Man in the Garden

Green man in the garden
　　Staring from the tree,
Why do you look so long and hard
　　Through the pane at me?

Your eyes are dark as holly,
　　Of sycamore your horns,
Your bones are made of elder-branch,
　　Your teeth are made of thorns.

Your hat is made of ivy-leaf,
　　Of bark your dancing shoes,
And evergreen and green and green
　　Your jacket and shirt and trews.

Leave your house and leave your land
　　And throw away the key,
And never look behind, he creaked,
　　And come and live with me.

I bolted up the window,
　　I bolted up the door,
I drew the blind that I should find
　　The green man never more.

But when I softly turned the stair
　　As I went up to bed,
I saw the green man standing there.
　　'Sleep well, my friend,' he said.

The Reverend Sabine Baring-Gould

The Reverend Sabine Baring-Gould,
　　Rector (sometime) at Lew,
Once at a Christmas party asked,
　　'Whose pretty child are you?'

(The Rector's family was long,
　　His memory was poor,
And as to who was who had grown
　　Increasingly unsure.)

At this, the infant on the stair
　　Most sorrowfully sighed.
'Whose pretty little girl am I?
　　Why, *yours*, papa!' she cried.

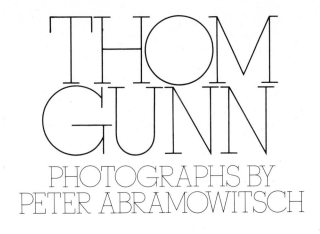

THOM GUNN

PHOTOGRAPHS BY PETER ABRAMOWITSCH

Thom Gunn was born at Gravesend in 1929 and educated at University
College School, London, and at Cambridge, where he **quickly grew up
after hearing someone suggest that Edith Sitwell was a bad poet.** In
1957 he said of himself: **I don't deliberately belong to any school, but
I suppose I am part of the National Service Generation and have a few
of its characteristics, i.e. lack of concern with religion, lack of class, a
rather undirected impatience.** He has travelled widely, in Italy and
America, and has taught in San Antonio, Texas, and Berkeley and
Stanford, California.

He has published *Fighting Terms* (1954), *The Sense of Movement*
(1957), *My Sad Captains* (1961), *Touch* (1967), *Moly* (1971) and
Poems 1950–1966: A Selection (1969).

My Suburban Muse

For most of my adolescence I lived in Hampstead, in the north west of
London. But during the Blitz I was evacuated to a school in the
country, where an enlightened English teacher taught from The Poet's
Tongue (edited by W. H. Auden and John Garrett). It was a remarkable
anthology to encounter in 1941, very different from the Dragon Book
of Verse, which you got in other schools, and which was all Lord
Macaulay and the patriotic speeches from Henry V. In the introduction to The Poet's Tongue poetry was defined as 'memorable speech',
still the only workable definition I've come across; and the anthology
itself emphasized the range and liveliness- of poetry, by including
mnemonics, popular songs, mummers' plays, nonsense poetry, songs
by Blake, medieval fragments, and at one point two haunting lines
from an Elegy of Donne's printed by themselves, as if they were a
whole poem:

Nurse oh My Love is slain, I saw him go
Oer the white alps alone.

Yet though I enjoyed the book I evidently had a more conventional
idea of the poetry I wanted to write. Returning to Hampstead at
thirteen I read some Greek myths and wrote a poem about a peony,
which started:

O peony you smell
Like the heavenly nectar Hebe spilt
On luxurious Olympus.

And about this time I fell for Keats – fell for him as you do for the
first poet who really means something to you. I read him all and liked

him all, without discrimination, having certain vague yearnings which his poetry answered very satisfactorily. 'I stood tiptoe upon a little hill' – why, it could be Hampstead Heath. In fact, it must have been, because Keats had lived in Hampstead, hadn't he? I doubt if it struck me that Keats's Hampstead had been a village surrounded by real countryside, whereas my Hampstead, though made quiet and almost rural by petrol rationing, was still a part of London – and London at war. If there were cuckoos in the big garden across the road for the last two summers of the war, there were also long convoys of army lorries coiling down Frognal, the houses designed by Freud's son were requisitioned for troops, GIs drank in the William IV and the Flask, and the public library was hit by a V2.

But I found all this easy enough to forget when I was on the Heath. I am still easily moved by the enclosed greenery of parks – as if its being seen by so many humans had brushed off onto it certain slightly human qualities, ranging from the poignant to the sinister. Anyway, for me Hampstead Heath became poeticized by Keats. I particularly liked the view from Judge's Walk; you could gaze from the hill into a distance as brilliantly hazy as it is in Turner's Crossing the Brook, which was one of my favourite pictures. I disregarded that what the haze covered was actually only the London suburb of Golders Green. What I encouraged in my poetry, indeed, was less the sharp-eyed exactness of Keats than an air of vague and nebulous beauty that concealed the actual world very nicely. I was prepared to write about a hazy distance of spire and rooftop, but not Golders Green.

I remember I wrote a poem about Eel Pie Island, at Richmond, a compact and pretty place with banks held in by mossy boards, and covered by trees which bulged out romantically over the Thames. But the island I wrote about only took this as its starting point: in the poem it rapidly filled up with ivy-festooned statues of Greek gods and goddesses.

I enjoyed Marlowe and Beddoes and then, when I was seventeen, Meredith. I carried a small red book of Meredith's poetry in my pocket for several months, and read from it so often that I knew some of it by heart. My favourite was 'Love in the Valley', which began:

Under yonder beechtree, single in the greensward,
Couched with her arms beneath her golden head,
Knees and tresses folded to slip and ripple idly,
My young love lies sleeping in the shade.
Had I the heart to slide an arm beneath her,
Press her parting lips as her waist I gather slow,
Waking in amazement she could not but embrace me:
Then would she hold me and never let me go?

I can certainly see the attraction of that metre, but I must say the language is quite a step down from Keats. However, it corresponded to what I now wanted in poetry, and seemed to me positively reckless in its sexiness. One evening in the tube, about this time, I noticed that a rather pretty girl was looking at me, and our eyes met. She was probably merely observing the state of my acne, and of course I never saw her again, but that was all to the good, since I could now imagine her whatever I wanted. The instant, looked back upon, became marked as a memorable lost opportunity. My walks on the Heath became longer and more melancholy. I wrote a poem beginning:

We lay upon a furzy, fire-dry bank
Where green was withered by our passion's flame,
And as there came an ecstasy we drank
Searing salt kisses that quenched not when they came,
Searing salt kisses that quenched not when they came.

I don't remember how it went on (was there anything, indeed, left to add?), but I must have liked that stanza a good deal to be able to write it out from memory twenty-six years later. I was particularly proud of the repeated last line.

I am not trying to sneer at my seventeen-year-old self. Like most people at that age, I had a lot of deep feeling hanging around and didn't quite know what to connect it with. But at least I was trying to do something about it, to assign it some kind of meaning, attach it to something outside of me, even if I wasn't doing it very well. And the poetry I was writing strikes me as constituting a beginning that was perfectly legitimate, and in itself perfectly valueless, like most literary beginnings. I say legitimate, in that it seemed to involve a commitment to writing, and so if I was lucky it might lead somewhere, even though it was all based on illusion and fantasy.

What trite adolescent dreams of being loved by a demonic hero are behind Wuthering Heights, what visions of being a dashing young soldier annihilating enemies in battle and breaking hearts in the drawing room are behind Stendhal's novels? Fantasy must always precede fictions, and fictions are as necessary as reality to literature. Love poetry started as the fantasies of troubadours, who by definition had to love at a distance. You can't get the girl you want, so you create a fantasy about her so complete that it can give you some temporary satisfaction. Later I had for a while a theory of poetry as 'loot', a prize grabbed from the outside world and taken permanently into the poet's possession. But of course it isn't taken, it continues out there in the world living its own independent existence, stepping from the tube-train at a later stop, and coolly unaware of all the furore it is causing.

My poems, then, were intensely felt and intensely derivative. At

least the intensity was there. What I had to learn was to free myself
from too limited a notion of the poetic. I might have had it from The
Poet's Tongue; that all experience, including Golders Green and acne,
is suitable to poetry. But I had to find that out for myself when I was
ready. And I would not be ready till I was in my twenties.

Last year I wrote the following poem, about what qualities I'd want
to get into an autobiography, if I were to write one. It can be read as a
comment, of sorts, on what I've been speaking about.

Autobiography

The sniff of the real, that's
what I'd want to get
      how it felt
to sit on Parliament
Hill on a May evening
studying for exams   skinny
seventeen   dissatisfied
      yet sniffing such
a potent air, smell of
grass in heat from
the day's sun

I'd been walking through the damp
rich ways by the ponds
and now lay on the upper
grass with Lamartine's poems

life seemed all
loss, and what was more
I'd lost whatever it was
before I'd even had it

a green dry prospect
distant babble of children
and beyond, distinct at
the end of the glow
St Paul's like a stone thimble

longing so hard to make
inclusions that the longing
has become   in memory
an inclusion

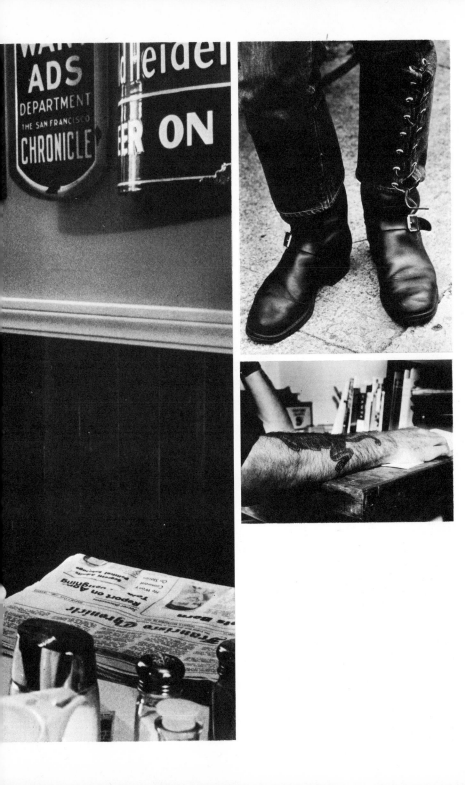

Tamer and Hawk

I thought I was so tough,
But gentled at your hands
Cannot be quick enough
To fly for you and show
That when I go I go
At your commands.

Even in flight above
I am no longer free:
You seeled me with your love,
I am blind to other birds –
The habit of your words
Has hooded me.

As formerly, I wheel
I hover and I twist,
But only want the feel
In my possessive thought,
Of catcher and of caught
Upon your wrist.

You but half-civilize,
Taming me in this way.
Through having only eyes
For you I fear to lose,
I lose to keep, and choose
Tamer as prey.

Incident on a Journey

One night I reached a cave: I slept, my head
Full of the air. There came about daybreak
A red-coat soldier to the mouth, who said
'I am not living, in hell's pains I ache,
    But I regret nothing.'

His forehead had a bloody wound whose streaming
The pallid staring face illuminated.
Whether his words were mine or his, in dreaming
I found they were my deepest thoughts translated.
    '*I regret nothing:*

'Turn your closed eyes to see upon these walls
A mural scratched there by an earlier man,
And coloured with the blood of animals:
Showing humanity beyond its span,
    Regretting nothing.

'No plausible nostalgia, no brown shame
I had when treating with my enemies.
And always when a living impulse came
I acted, and my action made me wise.
    And I regretted nothing.

'I as possessor of unnatural strength
Was hunted, one day netted in a brawl;
A minute far beyond a minute's length
Took from me passion, strength, and life, and all.
    But I regretted nothing.

'Their triumph left my body in the dust;
The dust and beer still clotting in my hair
When I rise lonely, will-less. Where I must
I go, and what I must I bear.
    And I regret nothing.

'My lust runs yet and is unsatisfied,
My hate throbs yet but I am feeble-limbed;
If as an animal I could have died
My death had scattered instinct to the wind,
    Regrets as nothing.'

Later I woke. I started to my feet.
The valley light, the mist already going.
I was alive and felt my body sweet,
Uncaked blood in all its channels flowing.
    I would regret nothing.

On the Move
'Man, you gotta Go.'

The blue jay scuffling in the bushes follows
Some hidden purpose, and the gust of birds
That spurts across the field, the wheeling swallows,
Have nested in the trees and undergrowth.
Seeking their instinct, or their poise, or both,
One moves with an uncertain violence
Under the dust thrown by a baffled sense
Or the dull thunder of approximate words.

On motorcycles, up the road, they come:
Small, black, as flies hanging in heat, the Boys,
Until the distance throws them forth, their hum
Bulges to thunder held by calf and thigh.
In goggles, donned impersonality,
In gleaming jackets trophied with the dust,
They strap in doubt – by hiding it, robust –
And almost hear a meaning in their noise.

Exact conclusion of their hardiness
Has no shape yet, but from known whereabouts
They ride, direction where the tires press.
They scare a flight of birds across the field:
Much that is natural, to the will must yield.
Men manufacture both machine and soul,
And use what they imperfectly control
To dare a future from the taken routes.

It is a part solution, after all.
One is not necessarily discord
On earth; or damned because, half animal,
One lacks direct instinct, because one wakes
Afloat on movement that divides and breaks.
One joins the movement in a valueless world,
Choosing it, till, both hurler and the hurled,
One moves as well, always toward, toward.

A minute holds them, who have come to go:
The self-defined, astride the created will
They burst away; the towns they travel through
Are home for neither bird nor holiness,
For birds and saints complete their purposes.
At worst, one is in motion; and at best,
Reaching no absolute, in which to rest,
One is always nearer by not keeping still.
California

The Discovery of the Pacific

They lean against the cooling car, backs pressed
Upon the dusts of a brown continent,
And watch the sun, now Westward of their West,
Fall to the ocean. Where it led they went.

Kansas to California. Day by day
They travelled emptier of the things they knew.
They improvised new habits on the way,
But lost the occasions, and then lost them too.

One night, no-one and nowhere, she had woken
To resin-smell and to the firs' slight sound,
And through their sleeping-bag had felt the broken
Tight-knotted surfaces of the naked ground.

Only his lean quiet body cupping hers
Kept her from it, the extreme chill. By degrees
She fell asleep. Around them in the firs
The wind probed, tiding through forked estuaries.

And now their skin is caked with road, the grime
Merely reflecting sunlight as it fails.
They leave their clothes among the rocks they climb,
Blunt leaves of iceplant nuzzle at their soles.

Now they stand chin-deep in the sway of ocean,
Firm West, two stringy bodies face to face,
And come, together, in the water's motion,
The full caught pause of their embrace.

Listening to Jefferson Airplane
in the Polo Grounds, Golden Gate Park

The music comes and goes on the wind,
Comes and goes on the brain.

The Unsettled Motorcyclist's Vision of His Death

Across the open countryside,
Into the walls of rain I ride.
It beats my cheek, drenches my knees,
But I am being what I please.

The firm heath stops, and marsh begins.
Now we're at war: whichever wins
My human will cannot submit
To nature, though brought out of it.
The wheels sink deep; the clear sound blurs:
Still, bent on the handle-bars,
I urge my chosen instrument
Against the mere embodiment.
The front wheel wedges fast between
Two shrubs of glazed insensate green
– Gigantic order in the rim
Of each flat leaf. Black eddies brim
Around my heel which, pressing deep,
Accelerates the waiting sleep.

I used to live in sound, and lacked
Knowledge of still or creeping fact.
But now the stagnant strips my breath,
Leant on my cheek in weight of death.
Though so oppressed I find I may
Through substance move. I pick my way,
Where death and life in one combine,
Through the dark earth that is not mine,
Crowded with fragments, blunt, unformed;
While past my ear where noises swarmed
The marsh plant's white extremities,
Slow without patience, spread at ease
Invulnerable and soft, extend
With a quiet grasping toward their end.

And though the tubers, once I rot,
Reflesh my bones with pallid knot,
Till swelling out my clothes they feign
This dummy is a man again,
It is as servants they insist,
Without volition that they twist;
And habit does not leave them tired,
By men laboriously acquired.
Cell after cell the plants convert
My special richness in the dirt:
All that they get, they get by chance.

And multiply in ignorance.

Apartment Cats

The Girls wake, stretch, and pad up to the door.
    They rub my leg and purr:
    One sniffs around my shoe,
    Rich with an outside smell,
  The other rolls back on the floor –
White bib exposed, and stomach of soft fur.

Now, more awake, they re-enact Ben Hur
    Along the corridor,
    Wheel, gallop; as they do,
    Their noses twitching still,
  Their eyes get wild, their bodies tense,
Their usual prudence seemingly withdraws.

And then they wrestle: parry, lock of paws,
    Blind hug of close defence,
    Tail-thump, and smothered mew.
    If either, though, feel claws,
  She abruptly rises, knowing well
How to stalk off in wise indifference.

The Produce District
What's there to do on Sundays? Sooner do this than booze.

After the businesses had moved, before
The wrecking started
For the high-rise blocks:
An interim:
Whoever walked along these streets
Found it was shared with him
Only by pigeons, single or in flocks.

Where each night trucks had waited
By warehouse and worn ramp
With oranges or celery to unload,
Now it was smell of must, rot, fungus, damp.
The crumbling and decay accelerated,
Old mattresses and boards in heaps
Losing their colours with their shapes,
The smaller things
Blending like humus, on the road.
And silence – no, small creaks,
Small patterings,
While now, above, the thump and whirr of wings.
The pigeons, grey on grey,
In greater number
Than ever here before
Pecked round the rotting lumber,
Perched on the roofs and walls,
Or wheeled between the faded signs
And broken ornamental scrolls.

I watched the work of spiders, rats, and rain,
And turning on to Front Street found
I was not there alone.
He stood unmoving on the littered ground
In bright scrubbed denims
An airgun loosely in his hands
Staring at something overhead.

Shooting at birds, he said.
I looked at his short greying hair;
His face, lined, hard and ruddy, any age,
Cracking into a smile;
And stood beside him while
He aimed at a parapet some forty-five yards off.
A bang. One pigeon as the others rose
A lump of fluff
Dropped from among them lightly to the street.

Cool air, high fog, and underfoot
Through soft mould, shapes felt like uneven root
Ridging a forest floor.
The place losing itself, lost now, unnamed,
Birds wheeling back, with a low threshing sound.
He aimed
And then once more
I heard the gun repeat
Its accurate answer to the wilderness,
Echoing it and making it complete.
And maple shoots pushed upward through the ground.

Taylor Street

The small porch of imitation
marble is never sunny, but
outside the front door he
sits on his kitchen chair facing
the street. In the bent yellowish
face, from under the brim
of a floppy brown hat,
his small eyes watch what
he is not living. But he
lives what he can:
watches without a smile, with
a certain strain, the warmth
of his big crumpled
body anxiously cupped
by himself in himself, as
he leans over himself not
over the cold railing, unmoving but carefully getting
a little strength from the sight of the
passers-by. He has it
all planned: he will live
here morning by morning.

Epitaph for Anton Schmidt
(from *Misanthropos*)

The Schmidts obeyed, and marched on Poland.
And there an Anton Schmidt, Feldwebel,
Performed uncommon things, not safe,
Nor glamorous, nor profitable.

Was the expression on his face
'Reposeful and humane good nature'?
Or did he look like any Schmidt,
Of slow and undisclosing feature?

I know he had unusual eyes,
Whose power no orders might determine,
Not to mistake the men he saw,
As others did, for gods or vermin.

For five months, till his execution,
Aware that action has its dangers,
He helped the Jews to get away
– Another race at that, and strangers.

He never did mistake for bondage
The military job, the chances,
The limits; he did not submit
To the blackmail of his circumstances.

I see him in the Polish snow,
His muddy wrappings small protection,
Breathing the cold air of his freedom
And treading a distinct direction.

Innocence
(to Tony White)

He ran the course and as he ran he grew,
And smelt his fragrance in the field. Already,
Running he knew the most he ever knew,
The egotism of a healthy body.

Ran into manhood, ignorant of the past:
Culture of guilt and guilt's vague heritage,
Self-pity and the soul; what he possessed
Was rich, potential, like the bud's tipped rage.

The Corps developed, it was plain to see,
Courage, endurance, loyalty and skill
To a morale firm as morality,
Hardening him to an instrument, until

The finitude of virtues that were there
Bodied within the swarthy uniform
A compact innocence, child-like and clear,
No doubt could penetrate, no act could harm.

When he stood near the Russian partisan
Being burned alive, he therefore could behold
The ribs wear gently through the darkening skin
And sicken only at the Northern cold,

Could watch the fat burn with a violet flame
And feel disgusted only at the smell,
And judge that all pain finishes the same
As melting quietly by his boots it fell.

My Sad Captains

One by one they appear in
the darkness: a few friends, and
a few with historical
names. How late they start to shine!
but before they fade they stand
perfectly embodied, all

the past lapping them like a
cloak of chaos. They were men
who, I thought, lived only to
renew the wasteful force they
spent with each hot convulsion.
They remind me, distant now.

True, they are not at rest yet,
but now that they are indeed
apart, winnowed from failures,
they withdraw to an orbit
and turn with disinterested
hard energy, like the stars.

Claus Von Stauffenberg
of the bomb-plot on Hitler, 1944

What made the place a landscape of despair,
History stunned beneath, the emblems cracked?
Smell of approaching snow hangs on the air;
The frost meanwhile can be the only fact.

They chose the unknown, and the bounded terror,
As a corrective, who corrected live
Surveying without choice the bounding error:
An unsanctioned present must be primitive.

A few still have the vigour to deny
Fear is a natural state; their motives neither
Of doctrinaire, of turncoat, nor of spy.
Lucidity of thought draws them together.

The maimed young Colonel who can calculate
On two remaining fingers and a will,
Takes lessons from the past, to detonate
A bomb that Brutus rendered possible.

Over the maps a moment, face to face:
Across from Hitler, whose grey eyes have filled
A nation with the illogic of their gaze,
The rational man is poised, to break, to build.

And though he fails, honour personified
In a cold time where honour cannot grow,
He stiffens, like a statue, in mid-stride
– Falling toward history, and under snow.

Flying Above California

Spread beneath me it lies – lean upland
sinewed and tawny in the sun, and

valley cool with mustard, or sweet with
loquat. I repeat under my breath

names of places I have not been to:
Crescent City, San Bernardino

– Mediterranean and Northern names.
Such richness can make you drunk. Sometimes

on fogless days by the Pacific,
there is a cold hard light without break

that reveals merely what is – no more
and no less. That limiting candour,

that accuracy of the beaches,
is part of the ultimate richness.

Considering the Snail

The snail pushes through a green
night, for the grass is heavy
with water and meets over
the bright path he makes, where rain
has darkened the earth's dark. He
moves in a wood of desire,

pale antlers barely stirring
as he hunts. I cannot tell
what power is at work, drenched there
with purpose, knowing nothing.
What is a snail's fury? All
I think is that if later

I parted the blades above
the tunnel and saw the thin
trail of broken white across
litter, I would never have
imagined the slow passion
to that deliberate progress.

'Blackie, the Electric Rembrandt'

We watch through the shop-front while
Blackie draws stars – an equal

concentration on his and
the youngster's faces. The hand

is steady and accurate;
but the boy does not see it

for his eyes follow the point
that touches (quick, dark movement!)

a virginal arm beneath
his rolled sleeve: he holds his breath.

. . . Now that it is finished, he
hands a few bills to Blackie

and leaves with a bandage on
his arm, under which gleam ten

stars, hanging in a blue thick
cluster. Now he is starlike.

Rites of Passage

Something is taking place.
Horns bud bright in my hair.
My feet are turning hoof.
And Father, see my face
– Skin that was damp and fair
Is barklike and, feel, rough.

See Greytop how I shine.
I rear, break loose, I neigh
Snuffing the air, and harden
Toward a completion, mine.
And next I make my way
Adventuring through your garden.

My play is earnest now.
I canter to and fro.
My blood, it is like light.
Behind an almond bough,
Horns gaudy with its snow,
I wait live, out of sight.

All planned before my birth
For you, Old Man, no other,
Whom your groin's trembling warns.
I stamp upon the earth
A message to my mother.
And then I lower my horns.

Second Take on *Rites of Passage*

Something is taking place.
Horns thrust upward from the brow.
Hooves beat impatient where feet once were.
My Son, youth grows alarming in your face.
Your innocent regard is cruelly charming to me now.
You bristle where my fond hand would stir
to stroke your cheek – I do not dare.

Irregular meters beat between your heart and mine.
Snuffling the air you take the heat and scan
the lines you take in going as if I were or were not there,
and overtake me, and where it seems but yesterday I spilld the wine,
you too grow beastly to become a man.

Peace, peace. I've had enough. What can I say
when song's demanded. I've had my fill of song?
My longing to sing grows full. Time's emptied me.

And where my youth was, now the Sun in you grows hot, your day
is young, my place you take triumphantly. All along,
it's been for you, for this lowering of your horns, She
had Her will of me and will not
    let my struggling spirit in itself be free.

Robert Duncan

Song

Fine knacks for ladies, cheap, choice, brave and new!
   Good pennyworths! but money cannot move.
I keep a fair but for the Fair to view;
   A beggar may be liberal of love.
Though all my wares be trash, the heart is true.

Great gifts are guiles and look for gifts again;
   My trifles come as treasures from my mind.
It is a precious jewel to be plain;
   Sometimes in shell the orient's pearls we find.
Of others take a sheaf, of me a grain.

Within this pack pins, points, laces, and gloves,
   And divers toys fitting a country fair,
But in my heart, where duty serves and loves,
   Turtles and twins, court's brood, a heavenly pair.
Happy the heart that thinks of no removes!

Set by John Dowland, possibly written by him.

Street Song

I am too young to grow a beard
But yes man it was me you heard
In dirty denim and dark glasses.
I look through everyone who passes
But ask him clear, I do not plead,
Keys lids acid and speed.

My grass is not oregano.
Some of it grew in Mexico.
You cannot guess the weed I hold,
Clara Green, Acapulco Gold,
Panama Red, you name it man,
Best on the street since I began.

My methedrine, my double-sun,
Will give you two lives in your one,
Five days of power before you crash.
At which time use these lumps of hash
– They burn so sweet, they smoke so smooth,
They make you sharper while they soothe.

Now here, the best I've got to show,
Made by a righteous cat I know.
Pure acid – it will scrape your brain,
And make it something else again.
Call it heaven, call it hell,
Join me and see the world I sell.

Join me, and I will take you there,
Your head will cut out from your hair
Into whichever self you choose.
With Midday Mick man you can't lose,
I'll get you anything you need.
Keys lids acid and speed.

SEAMUS HEANEY

PHOTOGRAPHS BY LARRY HERMAN

I was born in 1939 on a farm in County Derry, Ireland, and educated at St Columb's College, Derry, and Queen's University, Belfast. I began to write when I began to teach. I suppose I was stranded with myself and began taking stock in the poems.

His publications include: *Death of a Naturalist* (1966), *Door into the Dark* (1969) and *Wintering Out* (1972).

Singing-School

A few months ago I remembered a rhyme that we used to chant on the way to school. I know now that it is about initiation but as I trailed along the Lagan's Road on my way to Anahorish School it was something that was good for a laugh:

'Are your praties dry
And are they fit for digging?'
'Put in your spade and try,'
Says Dirty-Faced McGuigan.

I suppose I must have been about eight or nine years old when those lines stuck in my memory. They constitute a kind of poetry, not very respectable perhaps, but very much alive on the lips of that group of schoolboys, or 'scholars', as the older people were inclined to call us. McGuigan was probably related to a stern old character called Ned McGuigan who travelled the roads with a menacing blackthorn stick. He came from a district called Ballymacquigan – The Quigan, for short – and he turned up in another rhyme:

Neddy McGuigan,
He pissed in the Quigan;
The Quigan was hot
So he pissed in the pot;
The pot was too high
So he pissed in the sky;
Hell to your soul, Neddy McGuigan,
For pissing so high.

And there were other chants, scurrilous and sectarian, that we used to fling at one another:

Up the long ladder and down the short rope
To hell with King Billy and God bless the Pope.

Red, white and blue
Should be torn up in two
And sent to the devil
At half-past two.
Green, white and yellow
Is a decent fellow.

Another one which was completely nonsensical still pleases me:

One fine October's morning September last July
The moon lay thick upon the ground, the mud shone in the sky.
I stepped into a tramcar to take me across the sea,
I asked the conductor to punch my ticket and he punched my eye
                                                    for me.
I fell in love with an Irish girl, she sang me an Irish dance,
She lived in Tipperary, just a few miles out of France.
The house it was a round one, the front was at the back,
It stood alone between two more and it was whitewashed black.

We weren't forced to get these lines by heart. They just seemed to
spring in our mind and trip off the tongue spontaneously so that our
parents would say 'If it was your prayers, you wouldn't learn them
as fast'.

There were other poems, of course, that we were forced to learn by
heart. I am amazed to realize that at the age of eleven I was spouting
great passages of Byron and Keats by rote until the zinc roof of the
nissen hut that served for our schoolhouse (the previous school had
been cleared during the War to make room for an aerodrome) rang
to the half-understood magnificence of:

There was a sound of revelry by night
And Belgium's capital had gathered forth
Her beauty and her chivalry, and bright
The lamps shone over fair women and brave men.
A thousand hearts beat happily and when
The music rose with its voluptuous swell . . .

I also knew the whole of Keats's ode 'To Autumn' but the only line
that was luminous then was 'to bend with apples the mossed cottage
trees', because my uncle had a small orchard where the old apple-
trees were sleeved in a soft green moss. And I had a vague satisfaction
from 'the small gnats mourn/Among the river sallows', which would
have been complete if it had been 'midges' mourning among the
'sallies'.

The literary language, the civilized utterance from the classic canon of English poetry, was a kind of force-feeding. It did not delight us by reflecting our experience; it did not re-echo our own speech in formal and surprising arrangements. Poetry lessons, in fact, were rather like catechism lessons: official inculcations of hallowed formulae that were somehow expected to stand us in good stead in the adult life that stretched out ahead. Both lessons did indeed introduce us to the gorgeousness of the polysyllable, and as far as we were concerned there was little to choose between the music with 'its voluptuous swell' and the 'solemnization of marriage within forbidden degrees of consanguinity'. In each case we were overawed by the dimensions of the sound. (Maybe it was a genuine poetic experience after all.)

There was a third category of verse which I encountered at this time, half-way between the road-side rhymes and the school poetry (or 'poertry'), a form known to us as 'the recitation'. When relations visited or a children's party was held at home, I would be called upon to recite. Sometimes it would be an Irish patriotic ballad:

At length, brave Michael Dwyer, you and your trusty men
Were hunted o'er the mountain and tracked into the glen.
Sleep not, but watch and listen, keep ready blade and ball,
For the soldiers know you hide this night in the Glen of Wild Imall.

Sometimes, a western narrative by Robert Service:

A bunch of the boys were whooping it up in the Malamute Saloon.
The kid that handles the music-box was hitting a ragtime tune.
Back of the bar at a solo game sat Dangerous Dan Mulgrew
And watching his luck was his light o' love, the lady that's known
                                                              as Lou.

While this kind of stuff did not possess the lure of forbidden words like 'piss' and 'hell to your soul', it was not encumbered by the solemn incomprehensibility of Byron and Keats. It gave verse, however humble, a place in the life of the home, made it one of the ordinary rituals of life.

At the age of twelve I went to boarding school in St Columb's College, Derry. Old neighbours nodded wisely: 'The pen's lighter than the spade.' I was to be translated from the earth of physical labour to the heaven of education. Between that time and my graduation from Queen's University, Belfast, in 1961, I gradually grew more at ease in that poetic world which had eluded me in Anahorish School. Shakespeare, Chaucer, the Border ballads, Wordsworth, Hopkins, Arnold, Robert Frost – they were all part of 'the course' yet at different times I experienced real onsets of pleasure and epiphany in their work.

By the time I left St Columb's I had become acquainted with Latin
poetry as well and was passing notes in the study-hall in reasonable
Latin hexameters. I had also written a description of an old wall-stead
on our farm in Miltonic blank verse, although that was more for the
sake of parody than self-expression.

The alliterative poetry of Anglo-Saxon and Middle English, and the
dramatic poetry of Marlowe and Webster appealed to me at university.
The sensuous brunt of the words and metre, the sturdy collision between nature and art, the poetry's direct appeal to the nervous system
– I responded to this immediately, as I had responded to Hopkins's
consonantal lines that rang and ricocheted between the teeth and the
tongue. As an undergraduate I wrote a few poems, all of them
desperately imitative. This was my sub-Hopkins voice:

Starling thatch watches and sudden swallow
Straight breaks to mud-nest, home-rest rafter. . . .

More interesting to me than the poems is the pseudonym I used when
they appeared in the student magazine: I called myself 'Incertus', uncertain. Could I or couldn't I write a poem?

It was not until I began to teach in 1962 and began to read contemporary poetry – Patrick Kavanagh, Ted Hughes, R. S. Thomas
and the work of younger Irish poets like John Montague, Thomas
Kinsella and Richard Murphy – that I found my way to grafting
together the literary tradition I had studied and the life I had lived in
Co. Derry. By then my 'praties' were fit for 'Digging':

The cold smell of potato mould, the squelch and slap
Of soggy peat, the curt cuts of an edge
Through living roots awaken in my head.
But I've no spade to follow men like them.

Between my finger and my thumb
The squat pen rests.
I'll dig with it.

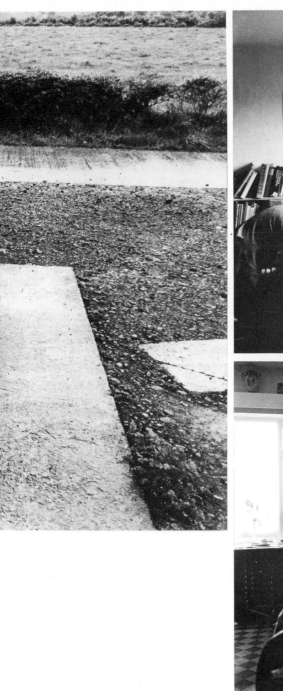

Digging

Between my finger and my thumb
The squat pen rests; snug as a gun.

Under my window, a clean rasping sound
When the spade sinks into gravelly ground:
My father, digging. I look down

Till his straining rump among the flowerbeds
Bends low, comes up twenty years away
Stooping in rhythm through potato drills
Where he was digging.

The coarse boot nestled on the lug, the shaft
Against the inside knee was levered firmly.
He rooted out tall tops, buried the bright edge deep
To scatter new potatoes that we picked
Loving their cool hardness in our hands.

By God, the old man could handle a spade.
Just like his old man.

My grandfather cut more turf in a day
Than any other man on Toner's bog.
Once I carried him milk in a bottle
Corked sloppily with paper. He straightened up
To drink it, then fell to right away
Nicking and slicing neatly, heaving sods
Over his shoulder, going down and down
For the good turf. Digging.

The cold smell of potato mould, the squelch and slap
Of soggy peat, the curt cuts of an edge
Through living roots awaken in my head.
But I've no spade to follow men like them.

Between my finger and my thumb
The squat pen rests.
I'll dig with it.

The Early Purges

I was six when I first saw kittens drown.
Dan Taggart pitched them, 'the scraggy wee shits',
Into a bucket; a frail metal sound,

Soft paws scraping like mad. But their tiny din
Was soon soused. They were slung on the snout
Of the pump and the water pumped in.

'Sure isn't it better for them now?' Dan said.
Like wet gloves they bobbed and shone till he sluiced
Them out on the dunghill, glossy and dead.

Suddenly frightened, for days I sadly hung
Round the yard, watching the three sogged remains
Turn mealy and crisp as old summer dung

Until I forgot them. But the fear came back
When Dan trapped big rats, snared rabbits, shot crows
Or, with a sickening tug, pulled old hens' necks.

Still, living displaces false sentiments
And now, when shrill pups are prodded to drown
I just shrug, 'Bloody pups'. It makes sense:

'Prevention of cruelty' talk cuts ice in town
Where they consider death unnatural,
But on well-run farms pests have to be kept down.

The Diviner

Cut from the green hedge a forked hazel stick
That he held tight by the arms of the V:
Circling the terrain, hunting the pluck
Of water, nervous, but professionally

Unfussed. The pluck came sharp as a sting.
The rod jerked down with precise convulsions,
Spring water suddenly broadcasting
Through a green aerial its secret stations.

The bystanders would ask to have a try.
He handed them the rod without a word.
It lay dead in their grasp till nonchalantly
He gripped expectant wrists. The hazel stirred.

Follower

My father worked with a horse-plough,
His shoulders globed like a full sail strung
Between the shafts and the furrow.
The horses strained at his clicking tongue.

An expert. He would set the wing
And fit the bright steel-pointed sock.
The sod rolled over without breaking.
At the headrig, with a single pluck

Of reins, the sweating team turned round
And back into the land. His eye
Narrowed and angled at the ground,
Mapping the furrow exactly.

I stumbled in his hob-nailed wake,
Fell sometimes on the polished sod;
Sometimes he rode me on his back
Dipping and rising to his plod.

I wanted to grow up and plough,
To close one eye, stiffen my arm.
All I ever did was follow
In his broad shadow round the farm.

I was a nuisance, tripping, falling,
Yapping always. But today
It is my father who keeps stumbling
Behind me, and will not go away.

Honeymoon Flight

Below, the patchwork earth, dark hems of hedge,
The long grey tapes of road that bind and loose
Villages and fields in casual marriage:
We bank above the small lough and farmhouse

And the sure green world goes topsy-turvy
As we climb out of our familiar landscape.
The engine noises change. You look at me.
The coastline slips away beneath the wing-tip.

And launched right off the earth by force of fire
We hang, miraculous, above the water,
Dependent on the invisible air
To keep us airborne and to bring us further.

Ahead of us the sky's a geyser now.
A calm voice talks of cloud yet we feel lost.
Air-pockets jolt our fears and down we go.
Travellers, at this point, can only trust.

Gone

Green froth that lathered each end
Of the shining bit
Is a cobweb of grass-dust.
The sweaty twist of the bellyband
Has stiffened, cold in the hand
And pads of the blinkers
Bulge through the ticking.
Reins, chains and traces
Droop in a tangle.

His hot reek is lost.
The place is old in his must.

He cleared in a hurry
Clad only in shods
Leaving this stable unmade.

The Salmon Fisher to the Salmon

The ridged lip set upstream, you flail
Inland again, your exile in the sea
Unconditionally cancelled by the pull
    Of your home water's gravity.

And I stand in the centre, casting.
The river cramming under me reflects
Slung gaff and net and a white wrist flicking
    Flies well-dressed with tint and fleck.

Walton thought garden worms, perfumed
By oil crushed from dark ivy berries
The lure that took you best, but here you come
    To grief through hunger in your eyes.

Ripples arrowing beyond me,
The current strumming water up my leg,
Involved in water's choreography
    I go, like you, by gleam and drag

And will strike when you strike, to kill.
We're both annihilated on the fly.
You can't resist a gullet full of steel.
    I will turn home fish-smelling, scaly.

The Forge

All I know is a door into the dark.
Outside, old axles and iron hoops rusting;
Inside, the hammered anvil's short-pitched ring,
The unpredictable fantail of sparks
Or hiss when a new shoe toughens in water.
The anvil must be somewhere in the centre,
Horned as a unicorn, at one end square,
Set there immovable: an altar
Where he expends himself in shape and music.
Sometimes, leather-aproned, hairs in his nose,
He leans out on the jamb, recalls a clatter
Of hoofs where traffic is flashing in rows;
Then grunts and goes in, with a slam and flick
To beat real iron out, to work the bellows.

Rite of Spring

So winter closed its fist
And got it stuck in the pump.
The plunger froze up a lump

In its throat, ice founding itself
Upon iron. The handle
Paralysed at an angle.

Then the twisting of wheat straw
Into ropes, lapping them tight
Round stem and snout, then a light

That sent the pump up in flame.
It cooled, we lifted her latch,
Her entrance was wet, and she came.

Undine

He slashed the briars, shovelled up grey silt
To give me right of way in my own drains
And I ran quick for him, cleaned out my rust.

He halted, saw me finally disrobed,
Running clear, with apparent unconcern.
Then he walked by me. I rippled and I churned

Where ditches intersected near the river
Until he dug a spade deep in my flank
And took me to him. I swallowed his trench

Gratefully, dispersing myself for love
Down in his roots, climbing his brassy grain –
But once he knew my welcome, I alone

Could give him subtle increase and reflection.
He explored me so completely, each limb
Lost its cold freedom. Human, warmed to him.

The Last Mummer

I

Carries a stone in his pocket,
an ash-plant under his arm.

Moves out of the fog
on the lawn, pads up the terrace.

The luminous screen in the corner
has them charmed in a ring

so he stands a long time behind them.
St George, Beelzebub and Jack Straw

can't be conjured from mist.
He catches the stick in his fist

and, shrouded, starts beating
the bars of the gate.

His boots crack the road. The stone
clatters down off the slates.

II

He came trammelled
in the taboos of the country

picking a nice way through
the long toils of blood

and feuding.
His tongue went whoring

among the civil tongues,
he had an eye for weather-eyes

at cross-roads and lane-ends
and could don manners

at a flutter of curtains.
His straw mask and hunch were fabulous

disappearing beyond the lamplit
slabs of a yard.

III

You dream a cricket in the hearth
and cockroach on the floor,

a line of mummers
marching out the door

as the lamp flares in the draught.
Melted snow off their feet

leaves you in peace.
Again an old year dies

on your hearthstone, for good luck.
The moon's host elevated

in a monstrance of holly trees,
he makes dark tracks, who had

untousled a first dewy path
into the summer grazing.

Toome

My mouth holds round
the soft blastings,
Toome, Toome,
as under the dislodged

slab of the tongue
I push into a souterrain
prospecting what new
in a hundred centuries'

loam, flints, musket-balls,
fragmented ware,
torcs and fish-bones
till I am sleeved in

alluvial mud that shelves
suddenly under
bogwater and tributaries,
and elvers tail my hair.

No Sanctuary

It's Hallowe'en. The turnip-man's lopped head
Blazes at us through split bottle glass
And fumes and swims up like a wrecker's lantern.

Death mask of harvest, mocker at All Souls
With scorching smells, red dog's eyes in the night –
We ring and stare into unhallowed light.

The Tollund Man

I

Some day I will go to Aarhus
To see his peat-brown head,
The mild pods of his eye-lids,
His pointed skin cap.

In the flat country nearby
Where they dug him out,
His last gruel of winter seeds
Caked in his stomach,

Naked except for
The cap, noose and girdle,
I will stand a long time.
Bridegroom to the goddess,

She tightened her torc on him
And opened her fen,
Those dark juices working
Him to a saint's kept body,

Trove of the turfcutters'
Honeycombed workings.
Now his stained face
Reposes at Aarhus.

II

I could risk blasphemy,
Consecrate the cauldron bog
Our holy ground and pray
Him to make germinate

The scattered, ambushed
Flesh of labourers,
Stockinged corpses
Laid out in the farmyards,

Tell-tale skin and teeth
Flecking the sleepers
Of four young brothers, trailed
For miles along the lines.

III
Something of his sad freedom
As he rode the tumbril
Should come to me, driving,
Saying the names

Tollund, Grabaulle, Nebelgard,
Watching the pointing hands
Of country people,
Not knowing their tongue.

Out there in Jutland
In the old man-killing parishes
I will feel lost,
Unhappy and at home.

Midnight

Since the professional wars –
Corpse and carrion
Paling in rain –
The wolf has died out

In Ireland. The packs
Scoured parkland and moor
Till a Quaker buck and his dogs
Killed the last one

In some scraggy waste of Kildare.
The wolfhound was crossed
With inferior strains,
Forests coopered to wine casks.

Rain on the roof to-night
Sogs turf-banks and heather,
Sets glinting outcrops
Of basalt and granite,

Drips to the moss of bare boughs.
The old dens are soaking.
The pads are lost or
Retrieved by small vermin

That glisten and scut.
Nothing is panting, lolling,
Vapouring. The tongue's
Leashed in my throat.

Bye-Child

*He was discovered in the henhouse
where she had confined him. He
was incapable of saying anything.*

When the lamp glowed,
A yolk of light
In their back window,
The child in the outhouse
Put his eye to a chink –

Little henhouse boy,
Sharp-faced as new moons
Remembered, your photo still
Glimpsed like a rodent
On the floor of my mind,

Little moon man,
Kennelled and faithful
At the foot of the yard,
Your frail shape, luminous,
Weightless, is stirring the dust,

The cobwebs, old droppings
Under the roosts
And dry smells from scraps
She put through your trapdoor
Morning and evening.

After those footsteps, silence;
Vigils, solitudes, fasts,
Unchristened tears,
A puzzled love of the light.
But now you speak at last

With a remote mime
Of something beyond patience,
Your gaping wordless proof
Of lunar distances
Travelled beyond love.

Augury

The fish faced into the current,
Its mouth agape,
Its whole head opened like a valve.
You said 'It's diseased.'

A pale crusted sore
Turned like a coin
And wound to the bottom,
Unsettling silt off a weed.

We hung charmed
On the trembling catwalk:
What can fend us now
Can soothe the hurt eye

Of the sun,
Unpoison great lakes,
Turn back
The rat on the road.

Westering
In California

I sit under Rand McNally's
'Official Map of the Moon' –
The colour of frogskin,
Its enlarged pores held

Open and one called
'Pitiscus' at eye level –
Recalling the last night
In Donegal, my shadow

Neat upon the whitewash
From her bony shine,
The cobbles of the yard
Lit pale as eggs.

Summer had been a free fall
Ending there,
The empty amphitheatre
Of the west. Good Friday

We had started out
Past shopblinds drawn on the afternoon,
Cars stilled outside still churches,
Bikes tilting to a wall;

We drove by,
A dwindling interruption
As clappers smacked
On a bare altar

And congregations bent
To the studded crucifix.
What nails dropped out that hour?
Roads unreeled, unreeled

Falling light as casts
Laid down
On shining waters.
Under the moon's stigmata

Six thousand miles away,
I imagine untroubled dust,
A loosening gravity,
Christ weighing by his hands.

Dedicatory Poem from **Wintering Out**
(for David Hammond and Michael Longley)

This morning from a dewy motorway
I saw the new camp for the internees:
a bomb had left a crater of fresh clay
in the roadside, and over in the trees

machine-gun posts defined a real stockade.
There was that white mist you get on a low ground
and it was déjà-vu, some film made
of Stalag 17, a bad dream with no sound.

Is there a life before death? That's chalked up
on a wall downtown. Competence with pain,
coherent miseries, a bite and sup,
we hug our little destiny again.

TED HUGHES

PHOTOGRAPHS BY
FAY GODWIN

Ted Hughes was born in 1930 at Mytholmroyd in the West Riding of Yorkshire, and educated at Mexborough Grammar School and Cambridge. He has worked variously as a gardener, a night-watchman and a reader at a film-studio. He has spent some time in America, but now lives in Devon.

His publications include *The Hawk in the Rain* (1957), *Lupercal* (1960), *The Earth-Owl and Other Moon-People* (1963), *Wodwo* (1967), *Crow* (1970) and a version of Seneca's *Oedipus*. His books for children include *The Iron Man* and *Meet My Folks!*

The Rock

The most impressive early companion of my childhood was a dark cliff, or what looked like a dark cliff, to the South, a wall of rock and steep woods half-way up the sky, just cleared by the winter sun. This was the memento mundi over my birth: my spiritual midwife at the time and my godfather ever since – or one of my godfathers. From my first day, it watched. If it couldn't see me direct, a towering gloom over my pram, it watched me through a species of periscope: that is, by infiltrating the very light of my room with its particular shadow. From my home near the bottom of the south-facing slope of the valley, that cliff was both the curtain and back-drop to existence. All that happened, happened against it or under its supervision. At the same time, all that I imagined happening elsewhere, out in the world, the rock sealed from me, since in England the world seems to lie to the South. If a man's death is held in place by a stone, my birth was fastened into place by that rock, and for my first seven years it pressed its shape and various moods into my brain. There was no easy way to escape it. I lived under it as under the presence of a war, or an occupying army: it constricted life in some way, demanded and denied, and was not happy. Beneath it, the narrow valley, with its flooring of cricket pitch, meadows, bowling greens, streets, railways and mills, seemed damp, dark and dissatisfied – dissatisfied because the east–west traffic poured through it on a main route, converting our town to a mere corridor between places of real importance, such as to the east, Halifax, with its formidable backing of Bradford, Huddersfield and Leeds, and to the west – after a grisly false start at Todmorden – Rochdale, backed by Manchester, Liverpool and New York. So while thinking distractedly out to east and west, we valley-dwellers were stuck looking at the dark hairy wall of Scout Rock, as it was called, and the final sensation was of having been trapped.

The oppression cast by that rock was a force in the minds of everyone there. I've heard that valley is notable for its suicides, which I can believe, and I could also believe that rock is partly to blame for them.

Most days it seems far enough off, deflated and scenic, with visible trees and scrambling walls to its steep fields, and clearly enough there is a farm or two along the top of it, people living happily up there and cattle grazing, and it's plainly no Eiger. But other days you step out of the house, or get off a bus come from elsewhere, and are astounded to see that blackish hogback mass riding directly overhead. Something about the clouds and light, the inclination of the season, or some overnight strengthening of the earth, has reared it right out over you, and you feel to be in the mouth of a vast dripping cave, in some hopeless age.

Now I think back I can't understand why I almost never went near it. I remember the pylons that stepped away toward the moors behind its left shoulder – these were the first pylons I ever saw at close quarters. And I was familiar with the road that draggled off among farms and cottages down behind its right shoulder into Luddenden Foot. But the steep face itself I never did encounter. The nearest I got was one memorable day I went up there with my brother, up one side, through the steep bracken and birches, and along the top where a thin path kept braving the very edge. Four things make that day memorable. First, the unique new view of the valley spread out below, from a wholly unimagined angle and from the other end of the telescope, as it were, up which I had gazed for about six years. I looked down at myself with the eye of the cliff, and that was a terrible piece of newness. Our house wasn't distinguishable. Too far off, too far below, in a tiny puzzle of houses. It was a balloon view. An alarming exhilaration. I felt infinitely exposed, to be up there on the stage I had been trying to imagine for so long. The second memorable detail was my discovery of oak-apples, in the little scrub oaks that twisted out their existence on the cliff-edge. It needed this spot-lit exalted rostrum to bring oak-apples to my notice, though I'd been seeing them all my life. Anyway, that's the first place I really concentrated on them with some surprise, and examined their corky interior and dusty worm-hole, and tossed them in numbers out into space, disappointing missiles, and put some in my pocket as if I might never find any again. And it was there that my brother told of a wood-pigeon shot in one of those little oaks, and how the bird set its wings and sailed out without a wing-beat stone dead into space to crash two miles away on the other side of the valley. And there followed the story of the tramp sleeping up there in the bracken, who stirred at an unlucky moment and was shot dead for a fox by an alert farmer and sent rolling down the slope. But of the rock-face, the central character to all that, I remember nothing, though I imagine I stared down it thoughtfully enough. That visit altered nothing, did nothing to tame the strangeness of my neighbour. I went on feeling it was alien, belonging to other people. I went on disliking it. It worked on me constantly. It should have inured me to living in valleys, or gulleys, or under walls, but all it did was cause me to hate them. The slightest declivity now makes me uneasy and restless, and I slip into the shadow of the mood of that valley – a foreboding heaviness, such as precedes downpour thunderstorms on Sunday afternoons. It's a mood that seems to have saturated the very stones of the walls and houses – those scorched-looking West Yorkshire grits – the pavements and the soil of the gardens and even the dark privet leaves. Most of all the dark privet leaves. A slightly disastrous crumbly grey light, sunless and yet too clear, like a still from the documentary film of an accident. The hours could be terribly long and empty, when the whole valley looked like a pre-first world war snapshot of itself, grey and faded, yet painfully bleak and irremovable, as if nobody could ever stir and nothing could ever happen there again. All because of that rock and its evil eye.

It had an evil eye, I've no doubt. For one thing you can't look at a precipice without thinking instantly what it would be like to fall down it, or jump down it. Mountaineers are simply men who need to counter-attack on that thought more forcibly than most people. But since Scout Rock was always there, that thought was always there – though you got used to it. It wasn't a frightening presence. It was a darkening presence, like an over-evident cemetery. Living beneath it was like living in a house haunted by a disaster that nobody can quite believe ever happened, though it regularly upsets sleep.

A not too remote line of my relatives farmed the levels above Scout Rock, for generations, in a black weepy farm that seemed to be made wholly of old gravestones and worn-out horse-troughs. Their survivors are still at it. And it was one of that family who once when he was out shooting rabbits on that difficult near-vertical terrain below his farm, not quite in living memory, took the plunge that the whole valley dreams about and fell to his death down the sheer face. A community peace-offering, I feel. An assurance, too, that the watchfully threatening aspect of the rock has something quite genuine about it. Recently a hoard of gold coins was unearthed at the foot of it, which has left the dark face with an even stranger expression.

Escape from the shadow trap was not east or west along the road – with the endless convoy of lorries loaded to the limit with bales of wool and bolts of cloth – but north and upwards, up the north slope to the moors. Ultimately, the valley was surrounded by moor skylines, further off and higher than the rock, folded one behind another. The rock asserted itself, tried to pin you down, policed and gloomed. But you could escape it, climb past it and above it, with some effort. You could not escape the moors. They did not impose themselves. They simply surrounded and waited. They were withdrawn, they hid behind their edges showing their possessions only upward, to the sky, and they preferred to be left alone, seeming almost to retreat as you approached them, lifting away behind one more slope of rough grass or parapet of broken stone. And however rarely you climbed to investigate them in detail, they hung over you at all times. They were simply a part of everything you saw. Whether you looked east, west, north or south, the earth was held down by that fine line of moor, mostly a gentle female watery line, moor behind moor, like a herd of enormous whales crowded all around at anchor. And just as the outlook of a bottle floating upright at sea consists of simple light and dark, the light above, the dark below, the two divided by a clear waterline, so my outlook was ruled by simple light and dark, divided by the undulating line of the moor. If any word could be found engraved around my skull, just above the ears and eyebrows, it would probably be the word 'horizon'. Every thought I tried to send beyond the confines of that valley had to step over that high definite hurdle. In most places the earth develops away naturally in every direction, over roads and crowded gradients and confused vistas, but there it rose up suddenly to a cut empty upturned edge, high in the sky, and stopped. I supposed it somehow started again somewhere beyond, with difficulty. So the visible horizon was the magic circle, excluding and enclosing, into which our existence had been conjured, and everything in me gravitated towards it.

I must have been quite young, three or four, when I started my walks to the moors. From the very start, the moors were the exciting destination. It was a long climb to get up there, and a thousand distractions tended to draw me off along the slope, among the woods and lanes and farms, but even if I wasted too much time in these ways, and had to turn back, I was reserving the moors as you do reserve the really superior pleasures, even from yourself.

The first half of the climb was over fields, and the first of these fields, two hundred yards above the house, was a mild domestic incline belonging to the Co-op, heavily grassed, usually pasturing a herd of cows. Coming up on to that, and turning back, you met Scout Rock opposite in its most formidable bluish aspect, over the slate roofs. The second field belonged to the farms above. It was poorer, wilder, steeper, and in it you began to feel a new sensation, the volume of space, the unaccustomed weight of open sky, and you saw that the ridge of Scout Rock was a ridge below the further ridge of moor, and moor was friendly. In the third much steeper field you began to feel bird-like, with sudden temptings to launch out in the valley air. From that field kites or gliders would stand out at a great height, and the traffic far below on the main road was like slow insects. Then the last fields rose in your face, and after almost a toiling stair you reached the farms, perched on knees of land or headlands, half-way up the valley sides. At that point you began to feel the spirit of the moors, the peculiar sad desolate spirit that cries in telegraph wires on moor roads, in the dry and so similar voices of grouse and sheep, and the moist voices of curlews. An avenue of tall trees ranged just above the first farm, I think sycamores, and the desolation of their foliage and silvery bark, the strange unearthly starkness of their attitudes, always struck me. I don't know quite what it was about them. Something of the sky moving so close above them, of the bleak black wall at the laneside, the scruffy gorse-tufted bulge of hillside just beyond. Or perhaps it was simply the light, at once both gloomily purplish and incredibly clear, unnaturally clear, as if objects there had less protection than elsewhere, were more exposed to the radio-active dangers of space, more startled by their own existence. But I liked that. In an imperfect reluctant way, these trees were beginning to reveal what showed nakedly in the ruined farms, with their one or two trees, along the moor's edge, or in the foul standing pools on the moor itself, and in the inane frozen looking eyes of the sheep. I sup-pose in some ways it was eerie, and maybe even unpleasant. But everything in West Yorkshire is slightly unpleasant. Nothing ever quite escapes into happiness. The people are not detached enough from the stone, as if they were only half-born from the earth, and the graves are too near the surface. A disaster seems to hang around in the air there for a long time. I can never escape the impression that the whole region is in mourning for the first world war. The moors don't escape this, but they give the sensation purely. And finally, in spite of it, the mood of moorland is exultant, and this is what I remember of it.

From there the return home was a descent into the pit, and after each visit I must have returned less and less of myself to the valley. This was where the division of body and soul, for me, began.

What do I write about?
After thinking the poems over, I have decided to say this: What excites my imagination is the war between vitality and death, and my poems may be said to celebrate the exploits of the warriors of either side. Also, they are attempts to prove the realness of the world, and of myself in this world, by establishing the realness of my relation to it. Another way of saying this might be – the poems celebrate the pure solidity of my illusion of the world. Again – and probably this is the first near-truth I have put down yet – they are the only way I can unburden myself of that excess which, for their part, bulls in June bellow away.

In each poem, besides the principal subject – and in my poems this is usually pretty easy to see, as, for instance, the jaguar in the poem called The Jaguar – there is what is not so easy to talk about, even generally, but which is the living and individual element in every poet's work. What I mean is the way he brings to peace all the feelings and energies which, from all over the body, heart, and brain, send up their champions onto the battleground of that first subject. The way I do this, as I believe, is by using something like the method of a musical composer. I might say that I turn every combatant into a bit of music, then resolve the whole uproar into as formal and balanced a figure of melody and rhythm as I can. When all the words are hearing each other clearly, and every stress is feeling every other stress, and all are contented – the poem is finished.

I have gone to some length, I see, to give what is perhaps a generalization about the composition of poetry, as well as a description of my own particular experience. I hope, though, to have defined the making of a special kind of verse. There is a great mass of English poetry in which the musical element – the inner figure of stress – is not so important as other elements. To me – no matter what metaphysical persuasion or definable philosophy a poem may seem to subscribe to – what is unique and precious in it is its heart, that inner figure of stresses. And in composing these poems I have been concerned to give to them – as well as good faces, clear brains and strong hands – sound hearts.

The Thought-Fox

I imagine this midnight moment's forest:
Something else is alive
Beside the clock's loneliness
And this blank page where my fingers move.

Through the window I see no star:
Something more near
Though deeper within darkness
Is entering the loneliness:

Cold, delicately as the dark snow
A fox's nose touches twig, leaf;
Two eyes serve a movement, that now
And again now, and now, and now

Sets neat prints into the snow
Between trees, and warily a lame
Shadow lags by stump and in hollow
Of a body that is bold to come

Across clearings, an eye,
A widening deepening greenness,
Brilliantly, concentratedly,
Coming about its own business

Till, with a sudden sharp hot stink of fox
It enters the dark hole of the head.
The window is starless still; the clock ticks,
The page is printed.

Song

O lady, when the tipped cup of the moon blessed you
You became soft fire with a cloud's grace;
The difficult stars swam for eyes in your face;
You stood, and your shadow was my place:
You turned, your shadow turned to ice
        O my lady.

O lady, when the sea caressed you
You were a marble of foam, but dumb.
When will the stone open its tomb?
When will the waves give over their foam?
You will not die, nor come home,
        O my lady.

O lady, when the wind kissed you
You made him music for you were a shaped shell.
I follow the waters and the wind still
Since my heart heard it and all to pieces fell
Which your lovers stole, meaning ill,
        O my lady.

O lady, consider when I shall have lost you
The moon's full hands, scattering waste,
The sea's hands, dark from the world's breast,
The world's decay where the wind's hands have passed,
And my head, worn out with love, at rest
In my hands, and my hands full of dust,
        O my lady.

The Jaguar

The apes yawn and adore their fleas in the sun.
The parrots shriek as if they were on fire, or strut
Like cheap tarts to attract the stroller with the nut.
Fatigued with indolence, tiger and lion

Lie still as the sun. The boa-constrictor's coil
Is a fossil. Cage after cage seems empty, or
Stinks of sleepers from the breathing straw.
It might be painted on a nursery wall.

But who runs like the rest past these arrives
At a cage where the crowd stands, stares, mesmerized,
As a child at a dream, at a jaguar hurrying enraged
Through prison darkness after the drills of his eyes

On a short fierce fuse. Not in boredom –
The eye satisfied to be blind in fire,
By the bang of blood in the brain deaf the ear –
He spins from the bars, but there's no cage to him

More than to the visionary his cell:
His stride is wildernesses of freedom:
The world rolls under the long thrust of his heel.
Over the cage floor the horizons come.

Wind

This house has been far out at sea all night,
The woods crashing through darkness, the booming hills,
Winds stampeding the fields under the window
Floundering black astride and blinding wet

Till day rose; then under an orange sky
The hills had new places, and wind wielded
Blade-light, luminous black and emerald,
Flexing like the lens of a mad eye.

At noon I scaled along the house-side as far as
The coal-house door. Once I looked up –
Through the brunt wind that dented the balls of my eyes
The tent of the hills drummed and strained its guyrope,

The fields quivering, the skyline a grimace,
At any second to bang and vanish with a flap:
The wind flung a magpie away and a black-
Back gull bent like an iron bar slowly. The house

Rang like some fine green goblet in the note
That any second would shatter it. Now deep
In chairs, in front of the great fire, we grip
Our hearts and cannot entertain book, thought,

Or each other. We watch the fire blazing,
And feel the roots of the house move, but sit on,
Seeing the window tremble to come in,
Hearing the stones cry out under the horizons.

Griefs for Dead Soldiers

I

Mightiest, like some universal cataclysm,
Will be the unveiling of their cenotaph:
The crowds will stand struck, like the painting of a terror
Where the approaching planet, a half-day off,
Hangs huge above the thin skulls of the silenced birds;
Each move, each sound, a fresh-cut epitaph –
Monstrousness of the moment making the air stone.

Though thinly, the bugle will then cry,
The dead drum tap, and the feet of the columns
And the sergeant-major's voice blown about by the wind
Make these dead magnificent, their souls
Scrolled and supporting the sky, and the national sorrow,
Over the crowds that know of no other wound,
Permanent stupendous victory.

II

Secretest, tiniest, there, where the widow watches on the table
The telegram opening of its own accord
Inescapably and more terribly than any bomb
That dives to the cellar and lifts the house. The bared
Words shear the hawsers of love that now lash
Back in darkness, blinding and severing. To a world
Lonely as her skull and little as her heart

The doors and windows open like great gates to a hell.
Still she will carry cups from table to sink.
She cannot build her sorrow into a monument
And walk away from it. Closer than thinking
The dead man hangs around her neck, but never
Close enough to be touched, or thanked even,
For being all that remains in a world smashed.

III

Truest, and only just, here, where since
The battle passed the grass has sprung up
Surprisingly in the valleyful of dead men.
Under the blue sky heavy crow and black fly move.
Flowers bloom prettily to the edge of the mass grave
Where spades hack, and the diggers grunt and sweat.
Among the flowers the dead wait like brides

To surrender their limbs; thud of another body flung
Down, the jolted shape of a face, earth into the mouth –
Moment that could annihilate a watcher!
Cursing the sun that makes their work long
Or the black lively flies that bite their wrists,
The burial party works with a craftsman calm.
Weighing their grief by the ounce, and burying it.

Six Young Men

The celluloid of a photograph holds them well, –
Six young men, familiar to their friends.
Four decades that have faded and ochre-tinged
This photograph have not wrinkled the faces or the hands.
Though their cocked hats are not now fashionable,
Their shoes shine. One imparts an intimate smile,
One chews a grass, one lowers his eyes, bashful,
One is ridiculous with cocky pride –
Six months after this picture they were all dead.

All are trimmed for a Sunday jaunt. I know
That bilberried bank, that thick tree, that black wall,
Which are there yet and not changed. From where these sit
You hear the water of seven streams fall
To the roarer in the bottom, and through all
The leafy valley a rumouring of air go.
Pictured here, their expressions listen yet,
And still that valley has not changed its sound
Though their faces are four decades under the ground.

This one was shot in an attack and lay
Calling in the wire, then this one, his best friend,
Went out to bring him in and was shot too;
And this one, the very moment he was warned
From potting at tin-cans in no-man's land,
Fell back dead with his rifle-sights shot away.
The rest, nobody knows what they came to,
But come to the worst they must have done, and held it
Closer than their hope; all were killed.

Here see a man's photograph,
The locket of a smile, turned overnight
Into the hospital of his mangled last
Agony and hours; see bundled in it
His mightier-than-a-man dead bulk and weight:
And on this one place which keeps him alive
(In his Sunday best) see fall war's worst
Thinkable flash and rending, onto his smile
Forty years rotting into soil.

That man's not more alive whom you confront
And shake by the hand, see hale, hear speak loud,
Than any of these six celluloid smiles are,
Nor prehistoric or fabulous beast more dead;
No thought so vivid as their smoking blood:
To regard this photograph might well dement,
Such contradictory permanent horrors here
Smile from the single exposure and shoulder out
One's own body from its instant and heat.

Crow Hill

The farms are oozing craters in
Sheer sides under the sodden moors:
When it is not wind it is rain,
Neither of which will stop at doors:
One will damp beds and the other shake
Dreams beneath sleep it cannot break.

Between the weather and the rock
Farmers make a little heat;
Cows that sway a bony back,
Pigs upon delicate feet
Hold off the sky, trample the strength
That shall level these hills at length.

Buttoned from the blowing mist
Walk the ridges of ruined stone.
What humbles these hills has raised
The arrogance of blood and bone,
And thrown the hawk upon the wind,
And lit the fox in the dripping ground.

A Dream of Horses

We were born grooms, in stable-straw we sleep still,
All our wealth horse-dung and the combings of horses,
And all we can talk about is what horses ail.

Out of the night that gulfed beyond the palace-gate
There shook hooves and hooves and hooves of horses:
Our horses battered their stalls; their eyes jerked white.

And we ran out, mice in our pockets and straw in our hair,
Into darkness that was avalanching to horses
And a quake of hooves. Our lantern's little orange flare

Made a round mask of our each sleep-dazed face,
Bodiless, or else bodied by horses
That whinnied and bit and cannoned the world from its place.

The tall palace was so white, the moon was so round,
Everything else this plunging of horses
To the rim of our eyes that strove for the shapes of the sound.

We crouched at our lantern, our bodies drank the din,
And we longed for a death trampled by such horses
As every grain of the earth had hooves and mane.

We must have fallen like drunkards into a dream
Of listening, lulled by the thunder of the horses.
We awoke stiff; broad day had come.

Out through the gate the unprinted desert stretched
To stone and scorpion; our stable-horses
Lay in their straw, in a hag-sweat, listless and wretched.

Now let us, tied, be quartered by these poor horses,
If but doomsday's flames be great horses,
The forever itself a circling of the hooves of horses.

Esther's Tomcat

Daylong this tomcat lies stretched flat
As an old rough mat, no mouth and no eyes.
Continual wars and wives are what
Have tattered his ears and battered his head.

Like a bundle of old rope and iron
Sleeps till blue dusk. Then reappear
His eyes, green as ringstones: he yawns wide red,
Fangs fine as a lady's needle and bright.

A tomcat sprang at a mounted knight,
Locked round his neck like a trap of hooks
While the knight rode fighting its clawing and bite.
After hundreds of years the stain's there

On the stone where he fell, dead of the tom:
That was at Barnborough. The tomcat still
Grallochs odd dogs on the quiet,
Will take the head clean off your simple pullet,

Is unkillable. From the dog's fury,
From gunshot fired point-blank he brings
His skin whole, and whole
From owlish moons of bekittenings

Among ashcans. He leaps and lightly
Walks upon sleep, his mind on the moon.
Nightly over the round world of men,
Over the roofs go his eyes and outcry.

Relic

I found this jawbone at the sea's edge:
There, crabs, dogfish, broken by the breakers or tossed
To flap for half an hour and turn to a crust
Continue the beginning. The deeps are cold:
In that darkness camaraderie does not hold:
Nothing touches but, clutching, devours. And the jaws,
Before they are satisfied or their stretched purpose
Slacken, go down jaws; go gnawn bare. Jaws
Eat and are finished and the jawbone comes to the beach:
This is the sea's achievement; with shells,
Vertebrae, claws, carapaces, skulls.

Time in the sea eats its tail, thrives, casts these
Indigestibles, the spars of purposes
That failed far from the surface. None grow rich
In the sea. This curved jawbone did not laugh
But gripped, gripped and is now a cenotaph.

Witches

Once was every woman the witch
To ride a weed the ragwort road;
Devil to do whatever she would:
Each rosebud, every old bitch.

Did they bargain their bodies or no?
Proprietary the devil that
Went horsing on their every thought
When they scowled the strong and lucky low.

Dancing in Ireland nightly, gone
To Norway (the ploughboy bridled),
Nightlong under the blackamoor spraddled,
Back beside their spouse by dawn

As if they had dreamed all. Did they dream it?
Oh, our science says they did.
It was all wishfully dreamed in bed.
Small psychology would unseam it.

Bitches still sulk, rosebuds blow,
And we are devilled. And though these weep
Over our harms, who's to know
Where their feet dance while their heads sleep?

Thrushes

Terrifying are the attent sleek thrushes on the lawn,
More coiled steel than living – a poised
Dark deadly eye, those delicate legs
Triggered to stirrings beyond sense – with a start, a bounce, a stab
Overtake the instant and drag out some writhing thing.
No indolent procrastinations and no yawning stares.
No sighs or head-scratchings. Nothing but bounce and stab
And a ravening second.

Is it their single-mind-sized skulls, or a trained
Body, or genius, or a nestful of brats
Gives their days this bullet and automatic
Purpose? Mozart's brain had it, and the shark's mouth
That hungers down the blood-smell even to a leak of its own
Side and devouring of itself: efficiency which
Strikes too streamlined for any doubt to pluck at it
Or obstruction deflect.

With a man it is otherwise. Heroisms on horseback,
Outstripping his desk-diary at a broad desk,
Carving at a tiny ivory ornament
For years: his act worships itself – while for him,
Though he bends to be blent in the prayer, how loud and above what
Furious spaces of fire do the distracting devils
Orgy and hosannah, under what wilderness
Of black silent waters weep.

Pike

Pike, three inches long, perfect
Pike in all parts, green tigering the gold.
Killers from the egg: the malevolent aged grin.
They dance on the surface among the flies.

Or move, stunned by their own grandeur,
Over a bed of emerald, silhouette
Of submarine delicacy and horror.
A hundred feet long in their world.

In ponds, under the heat-struck lily pads –
Gloom of their stillness:
Logged on last year's black leaves, watching upwards.
Or hung in an amber cavern of weeds

The jaws' hooked clamp and fangs
Not to be changed at this date;
A life subdued to its instrument;
The gills kneading quietly, and the pectorals.

Three we kept behind glass,
Jungled in weed: three inches, four,
And four and a half: fed fry to them –
Suddenly there were two. Finally one

With a sag belly and the grin it was born with.
And indeed they spare nobody.
Two, six pounds each, over two feet long,
High and dry and dead in the willow-herb –

One jammed past its gills down the other's gullet:
The outside eye stared: as a vice locks –
The same iron in this eye
Though its film shrank in death.

A pond I fished, fifty yards across,
Whose lilies and muscular tench
Had outlasted every visible stone
Of the monastery that planted them –

Stilled legendary depth:
It was as deep as England. It held
Pike too immense to stir, so immense and old
That past nightfall I dared not cast

But silently cast and fished
With the hair frozen on my head
For what might move, for what eye might move.
The still splashes on the dark pond,

Owls hushing the floating woods
Frail on my ear against the dream
Darkness beneath night's darkness had freed,
That rose slowly towards me, watching.

Second Glance at a Jaguar

Skinfull of bowl, he bowls them,
The hip going in and out of joint, dropping the spine
With the urgency of his hurry
Like a cat going along under thrown stones, under cover,
Glancing sideways, running
Under his spine. A terrible, stump-legged waddle
Like a thick Aztec disemboweller,
Club-swinging, trying to grind some square
Socket between his hind legs round,
Carrying his head like a brazier of spilling embers,
And the black bit of his mouth, he takes it
Between his back teeth, he has to wear his skin out,
He swipes a lap at the water-trough as he turns,
Swivelling the ball of his heel on the polished spot,
Showing his belly like a butterfly,
At every stride he has to turn a corner
In himself and correct it. His head
Is like the worn down stump of another whole jaguar,
His body is just the engine shoving it forward,
Lifting the air up and shoving on under,
The weight of his fangs hanging the mouth open,
Bottom jaw combing the ground. A gorged look,
Gangster, club-tail lumped along behind gracelessly,
He's wearing himself to heavy ovals,
Muttering some mantrah, some drum-song of murder
To keep his rage brightening, making his skin
Intolerable, spurred by the rosettes, the cain-brands,
Wearing the spots off from the inside,
Rounding some revenge. Going like a prayer-wheel,
The head dragging forward, the body keeping up,
The hind legs lagging. He coils, he flourishes
The blackjack tail as if looking for a target,
Hurrying through the underworld, soundless.

Wilfred Owen's Photographs

When Parnell's Irish in the House
Pressed that the British Navy's cat-
O-nine-tails be abolished, what
Shut against them? It was
Neither Irish nor English nor of that
Decade, but of the species.

Predictably, Parliament
Squared against the motion. As soon
Let the old school tie be rent
Off their necks, and give thanks, as see gone
No shame but a monument –
Trafalgar not better known.

'To discontinue it were as much
As ship not powder and cannonballs
But brandy and women' (Laughter). Hearing which
A witty profound Irishman calls
For a 'cat' into the House, and sits to watch
The gentry fingering its stained tails.

Whereupon . . .
                    quietly, unopposed,
The motion was passed.

Out

I
The Dream Time
My father sat in his chair recovering
From the four-year mastication by gunfire and mud,
Body buffeted wordless, estranged by long soaking
In the colours of multilation.
                            His outer perforations
Were valiantly healed, but he and the hearth-fire, its blood-flicker
On biscuit-bowl and piano and table-leg,
Moved into strong and stronger possession
Of minute after minute, as the clock's tiny cog
Laboured and on the thread of his listening
Dragged him bodily from under
The mortised four-year strata of dead Englishmen
He belonged with. He felt his limbs clearing
With every slight, gingerish movement. While I, small and four,
Lay on the carpet as his luckless double,
His memory's buried, immovable anchor,
Among jawbones and blown-off boots, tree-stumps, shell cases and craters,
Under rain that goes on drumming its rods and thickening
Its kingdom, which the sun has abandoned, and where nobody
Can ever again move from shelter.

II
The dead man in his cave beginning to sweat;
The melting bronze visor of flesh
Of the mother in the baby-furnace –
Nobody believes, it
Could be nothing, all
Undergo smiling at
The lulling of blood in
Their ears, their ears, their ears, their eyes
Are only drops of water and even the dead man suddenly
Sits up and sneezes – Atishoo!
Then the nurse wraps him up, smiling,
And, though faintly, the mother is smiling,
And it's just another baby.

As after being blasted to bits
The reassembled infantryman
Tentatively totters out, gazing around with the eyes
Of an exhausted clerk.

III
Remembrance Day
The poppy is a wound, the poppy is the mouth
Of the grave, maybe of the womb searching –

A canvas-beauty puppet on a wire
Today whoring everywhere. It is years since I wore one.

It is more years
The shrapnel that shattered my father's paybook

Gripped me, and all his dead
Gripped him to a time

He no more than they could outgrow, but, cast into one, like iron,
Hung deeper than refreshing of ploughs

In the woe-dark under my mother's eye –
One anchor

Holding my juvenile neck bowed to the dunkings of the Atlantic.
So goodbye to that bloody-minded flower.

You dead bury your dead.
Goodbye to the cenotaphs on my mother's breasts.

Goodbye to all the remaindered charms of my father's survival.
Let England close. Let the green sea-anemone close.

Pibroch

The sea cries with its meaningless voice
Treating alike its dead and its living,
Probably bored with the appearance of heaven
After so many millions of nights without sleep,
Without purpose, without self-deception.

Stone likewise. A pebble is imprisoned
Like nothing in the Universe.
Created for black sleep. Or growing
Conscious of the sun's red spot occasionally,
Then dreaming it is the foetus of God.

Over the stone rushes the wind
Able to mingle with nothing,
Like the hearing of the blind stone itself.
Or turns, as if the stone's mind came feeling
A fantasy of directions.

Drinking the sea and eating the rock
A tree struggles to make leaves –
An old woman fallen from space
Unprepared for these conditions.
She hangs on, because her mind's gone completely.

Minute after minute, aeon after aeon,
Nothing lets up or develops.
And this is neither a bad variant nor a tryout.
This is where the staring angels go through.
This is where all the stars bow down.

Gnat-Psalm

'The Gnat is of more ancient lineage than man.'   *Proverb*

When the gnats dance at evening
Scribbling on the air, sparring sparely,
Scrambling their crazy lexicon,
Shuffling their dumb Cabala,
Under leaf shadow

Leaves only leaves
Between them and the broad swipes of the sun
Leaves muffling the dusty stabs of the late sun
From their frail eyes and crepuscular temperaments

Dancing
Dancing
Writing on the air, rubbing out everything they write
Jerking their letters into knots, into tangles
Everybody everybody else's yoyo

Immense magnets fighting around a centre

Not writing and not fighting but singing
That the cycles of this Universe are no matter
That they are not afraid of the sun
That the one sun is too near
It blasts their song, which is of all the suns
That they are their own sun
Their own brimming over
At large in the nothing
Their wings blurring the blaze
Singing

That they are the nails
In the dancing hands and feet of the gnat-god
That they hear the wind suffering
Through the grass
And the evening tree suffering

The wind bowing with long cat-gut cries
And the long roads of dust
Dancing in the wind
The wind's dance, the death-dance, entering the mountain
And the cowdung villages huddling to dust

But not the gnats, their agility
Has outleaped that threshold
And hangs them a little above the claws of the grass
Dancing
Dancing
In the glove shadows of the sycamore

A dance never to be altered
A dance giving their bodies to be burned

And their mummy faces will never be used

Their little bearded faces
Weaving and bobbing on the nothing
Shaken in the air, shaken, shaken
And their feet dangling like the feet of victims

O little Hasids
Ridden to death by your own bodies
Riding your bodies to death
You are the angels of the only heaven!

And God is an Almighty Gnat!
You are the greatest of all the galaxies!
My hands fly in the air, they are follies
My tongue hangs up in the leaves
My thoughts have crept into crannies

Your dancing

Your dancing

Rolls my staring skull slowly away into outer space.

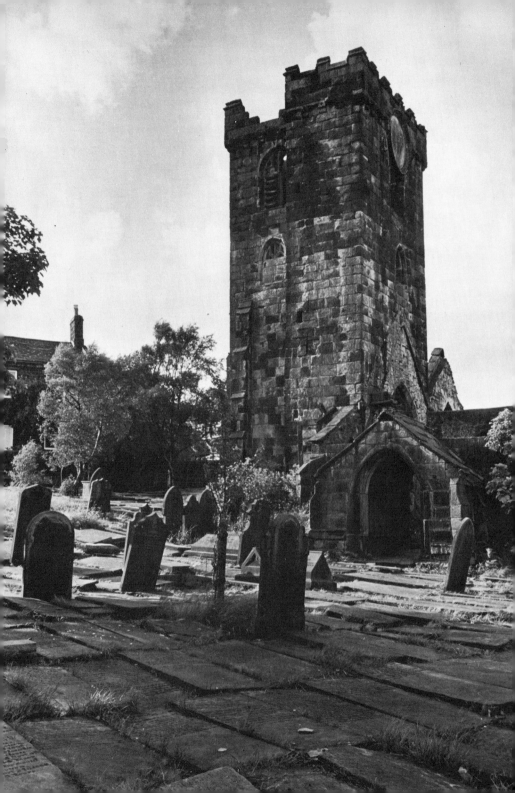

Heptonstall

Black village of gravestones.
Skull of an idiot
Whose dreams die back
Where they were born.

Skull of a sheep
Whose meat melts
Under its own rafters.
Only the flies leave it.

Skull of a bird,
The great geographies
Drained to sutures
Of cracked windowsills.

Life tries.

Death tries.

The stone tries.

Only the rain never tires.

Full Moon and Little Frieda

A cool small evening shrunk to a dog bark and the clank of a bucket –

And you listening.
A spider's web, tense for the dew's touch.
A pail lifted, still and brimming – mirror
To tempt a first star to a tremor.

Cows are going home in the lane there, looping the hedges with
                                    their warm wreaths of breath –
A dark river of blood, many boulders,
Balancing unspilled milk.

'Moon!' you cry suddenly, 'Moon! Moon!'

The moon has stepped back like an artist gazing amazed at a work
That points at him amazed.

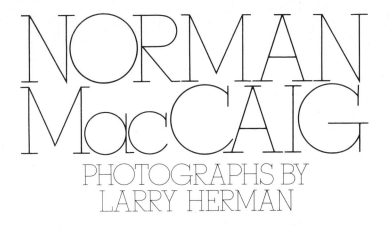

NORMAN MacCAIG

PHOTOGRAPHS BY LARRY HERMAN

Norman MacCaig was born in Edinburgh in 1910 and educated at Edinburgh University, where he read Classics. He earns his livelihood as a schoolmaster.

His publications include *Far Cry* (1943), *The Inward Eye* (1946), *Riding Lights* (1955), *The Sinai Sort* (1957), *A Common Grace* (1960), *A Round of Applause* (1962), *Measures* (1965), *Surroundings* (1966), *Rings on a Tree* (1968), *A Man in My Position* (1969) and *The White Bird* (1973).

If your parents and your grandparents, way back, all had red hair, it's likely yours will blaze away in the ancestral manner. But heredity doesn't seem to work with artists. Usually only one perches singing in his genealogical tree (though think of the incredible Bach family, an orchestra in themselves). As far as I know, I'm the only MacCaig ever to have committed poetry.

Everybody likes to make something, something that never existed before, whether it's a chair, a sand-pie, or a poem. I don't know what makes one man produce a poem and another man a chair; but I'm sure the creative instinct behind their activities is the same. If I made a chair, pity whoever would sit in it; and if the chairmaker produced a poem it would let you down too. But we're up to the same thing. If the creative processes that result in a poem are mysterious, they're no more mysterious than those that produce a chair. Their aim is to make something at once beautiful and useful.

Useful? It's easy to see that chairs come in handy. But what use is poetry?

It trains, educates, extends the range of our sensibility, as science and technology train the intellect. That's to say, the arts induce us to respond to and examine the emotional significance as well as the rational significance of whatever comes under our notice, and to have unexamined emotional responses is as much a sign of immaturity as to have unexamined beliefs. Now, an adult physique with the intelligence of a child is looked after. It might, some day, put an axe in somebody's skull. An adult intelligence with the emotional equipment of a child is just as dangerous: maybe more.

The chairmaker makes his chairs from whatever wood is available and so do I, only my wood is ideas, feelings, people and landscapes – particularly the astonishing assembly of shapes that make up Edinburgh, my home town, and the (to me) most seductive part of Scotland, that lies in the North-West, around the village of Lochinver. But of course one is influenced by, simply, everything. For the senses, the 'five ports of knowledge', are hospitable to everything, and into them sail, with luck, the most remarkable cargoes.

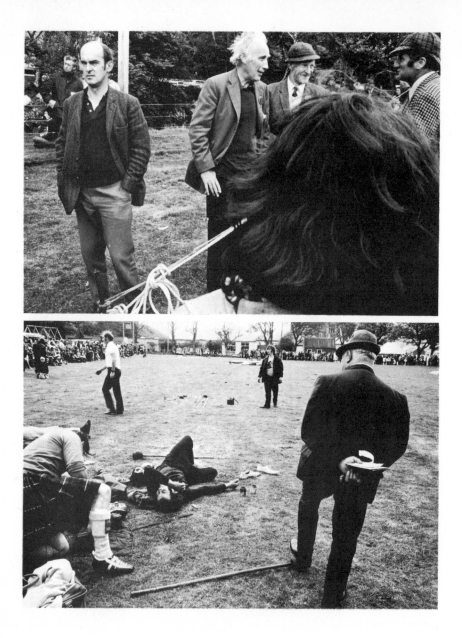

from No End, No Beginning

. . . But when was there a beginning
Of this turbulent love
For a sea shaking with light
And lullabying ditchwater
And a young twig being grave
Against constellations – these –
And people, invisibly webbing
Countries and continents,
Weeping, laughing, being idle
And always, always
Moving from light to darkness and
To light . . .

Byre

The thatched roof rings like heaven where mice
Squeak small hosannahs all night long,
Scratching its golden pavements, skirting
The gutter's crystal river-song.

Wild kittens in the world below
Glare with one flaming eye through cracks,
Spurt in the straw, are tawny brooches
Splayed on the chests of drunken sacks.

The dimness becomes darkness as
Vast presences come mincing in,
Swagbellied Aphrodites, swinging
A silver slaver from each chin.

And all is milky, secret, female.
Angels are hushed and plain straws shine.
And kittens miaow in circles, stalking
With tail and hindleg one straight line.

Visiting Hour

The hospital smell
combs my nostrils
as they go bobbing along
green and yellow corridors.

What seems a corpse
is trundled into a lift and vanishes
heavenward.

I will not feel, I will not
feel, until
I have to.

Nurses walk lightly, swiftly,
here and up and down and there,
their slender waists miraculously
carrying their burden
of so much pain, so
many deaths, their eyes
still clear after
so many farewells.

Ward 7. She lies
in a white cave of forgetfulness.
A withered hand
trembles on its stalk. Eyes move
behind eyelids too heavy
to raise. Into an arm wasted
of colour a glass fang is fixed,
not guzzling but giving.
And between her and me
distance shrinks till there is none left
but the distance of pain that neither she nor I
can cross.

She smiles a little at this
black figure in her white cave
who clumsily rises
in the round swimming waves of a bell
and dizzily goes off, growing fainter,
not smaller, leaving behind only
books that will not be read
and fruitless fruits.

Brooklyn Cop

Built like a gorilla but less timid,
thick-fleshed, steak-coloured, with two
hieroglyphs in his face that mean
trouble, he walks the sidewalk and the
thin tissue over violence. This morning
when he said, 'See you, babe' to his wife,
he hoped it, he truly hoped it.
He is a gorilla
to whom 'Hiya, honey' is no cliché.

Should the tissue tear, should he plunge through
into violence, what clubbings, what
gunshots between Phoebe's
Whamburger and Louie's Place.

Who would be him, gorilla with a nightstick,
whose home is a place
he might, this time, never get back to?

And who would be who have to be
his victims?

Basking Shark

To stub an oar on a rock where none should be,
To have it rise with a slounge out of the sea
Is a thing that happened once (too often) to me.

But not too often – though enough. I count as gain
That once I met, on a sea tin-tacked with rain,
That roomsized monster with a matchbox brain.

He displaced more than water. He shoggled me
Centuries back – this decadent townee
Shook on a wrong branch of his family tree.

Swish up the dirt and, when it settles, a spring
Is all the clearer. I saw me, in one fling,
Emerging from the slime of everything.

So who's the monster? The thought made me grow pale
For twenty seconds while, sail after sail,
The tall fin slid away and then the tail.

Wild Oats

Every day I see from my window
pigeons, up on a roof ledge – the males
are wobbling gyroscopes of lust.

Last week a stranger joined them, a snowwhite
pouting fantail,
Mae West in the Women's Guild.
What becks, what croo-croos, what
demented pirouetting, what a lack
of moustaches to stroke.

The females – no need to be one of them
to know
exactly what they were thinking – pretended
she wasn't there
and went dowdily on with whatever
pigeons do when they're knitting.

Old Maps and New

There are spaces
where infringements are possible.
There are notices that say:
Trespassers will be welcome.

Pity leaks through the roof
of the Labour Exchange.
In the Leader's pocket,
wrapped in the plans for the great offensive,
are sweets for the children
and a crumpled letter.

There are spaces still to be filled
before the map is completed –
though these days it's only
in the explored territories
that men write, sadly,
Here live monsters.

Odd Man Out

So green's my colour, though my country is
Gray stone, gray water.
(I hate a man who calls a country his.)

I watch red minds absolved from bodies go
In my gray weather,
Will-o'-the-wisping, fading as they glow.

Or bodies hulking hugely through the air
Mindlessly wander,
Shagging with browns and blues the grayness there.

Sometimes the bold sun, happening to pass by,
Blushes, just pinker,
The stone, the water and the drowning sky.

What's that to a man whose helpless knowledge is
Green is his colour?
(I hate a man who calls a colour his.)

So, like a bird that, perking up his song,
Denies it's winter,
I say green, green, green, green: and get along.

Frustrated Virtuoso

In the corner of Crombie's field
the donkey gets madder every minute. I listen
to his heehawing
seesawing and imagine
the round rich note
he wants to propel into space,
a golden planet of sound orbiting
to the wonder of the world.

No wonder
when he hears what comes out of
that whoopingcough trombone
his eyes fill with tears
and his box head drops
to lip the leaves of thistles – accepting that
they're all he deserves.

Moon-Landing

The rind of Newton's apple
was hard as a mason's hand;
yet the apple exploded, its pulp
spattered minds in closets
then minds outside closets.
That was the beginning.

Now two minds, hard
as silicon, glittering as quartz,
fall logically on moondust;
and blind stars and dwarf stars
are trees of apples and the forests
of galaxies make audible
their shaking leaves.
In a mind's midnight
they rustle and shine
as threatening as logic,
as beautiful as revelation.

New Tables

A mathematician who came to his senses
thought deeply
(putting his finger to his forehead,
putting his finger through his forehead)
and wrote:

One robust curse equals
two shrieks, four groans:
One hour with you
equals every convalescence:
One boy on a scooter equals
transport:
One Yes equals ten
commandments:
One new life equals
a million old deaths:
Love equals
equal.

The world read this, stupefied
with admiration
and went on dying and laughing
and shedding
logarithms of tears.

Blind Horse

He snuffles towards
pouches of water in the grass and doesn't drink
when he finds them.

He twitches listlessly at
sappy grass stems and stands
stone still, his hanging head
caricatured with a scribble
of green whiskers.

Sometimes that head swings high,
ears cock – and he stares
down a long sound, he stares and whinnies
for what never comes.

His eyes never close,
not in the heat of the day
when his leather lip droops and
he wears blinkers of flies.

At any time of the night
you hear him in his dark field
stamp the ground, stamp
the world down, waiting impatiently
for the light to break.

Beautiful Girl in a Gallery

Still life with vegetables
and you staring at it
so stilly.

The pigments in that still life
vibrate with
the intensity of their own being.
How could they do that
without light?

Stranger, I love you
standing so stilly
in the intensity of the light
you carry with you.

Boundaries

My summer thoughts, meek hinds, keep their own ground.
They graze and drowse and never think to roam
Beyond the pale of what they think is home –

A landscape with one fence, and that for deer.
Yet though it's seven feet high and so seems fit,
In winter snows they walk right over it.

Television Studio

Through an undersea growth
of flexes and cables,
three four-eyed monsters
prowl stealthily to and fro.
I know they're looking for me.

One stays still.   .
Cousteau'll be in that one.

Another, an angler fish,
reaches forward
a long antenna and dangles
a microphone before my face.

The three prowlers pause and
converge on me.
They stand in a terrible half-circle.

A green anemone lights up,
and from my mouth
learned bubbles emerge
as I give up the ghost
of what I had meant to say.

Aunt Julia

Aunt Julia spoke Gaelic
very loud and very fast.
I could not answer her –
I could not understand her.

She wore men's boots
when she wore any.
– I can see her strong foot,
stained with peat,
' paddling the treadle of the spinningwheel
while her right hand drew yarn
marvellously out of the air.

Hers was the only house
where I've lain at night
in the absolute darkness
of a box bed, listening to
crickets being friendly.

She was buckets
and water flouncing into them.
She was winds pouring wetly
round house-ends.
She was brown eggs, black skirts
and a keeper of threepenny bits
in a teapot.

Aunt Julia spoke Gaelic
very loud and very fast.
By the time I had learned
a little, she lay
silenced in the absolute black
of a sandy grave
at Luskentyre.
But I hear her still, welcoming me
with a seagull's voice
across a hundred yards
of peatscrapes and lazybeds
and getting angry, getting angry
with so many questions
unanswered.

Among the Talk and the Laughter

Why does he fall silent?
Why does that terrible, sad look
tell he has gone away?

He has died too often.
And something has been said
that makes him aware of the bodies
floating face downwards
in his mind.

Changes in the Same Thing

I'd seen her in stones
and behind rain and after minutes.
I'd spoken to her
in all the modes of silence, I'd measured her
with my eyelash thoughts.

Then she came: and was a hand
that took the place of everything –
till I saw her hair and it became
everywhere's nights and days – till
I saw the way she looked at me:
and I knew how Adam felt
when he woke from that deepest sleep
and, for the first time,
saw Her in the Garden.

Early Sunday Morning, Edinburgh

Crosshatch of streets: some waterfall
Down pits, some rear to lay their forepaws
On hilly ledges; others bore
Tunnels through lilac, gean and holly.

A stratch of sky makes what it can
Of ships sailing and sailing islands.
Trees open their rustling hands
And toss birds up, a fountain, a fanfare.

A yellow milkcart clipclops by
Like money shaken in a box,
Less yellow than the golden coxcomb
Gallanting on St Giles's spire.

And people idle into space
And disappear again in it –
Apparitions from nowhere: little
Sacraments shine from their faces.

And, fore and hindpaws out of line,
An old dog mooches by, his gold
Eyes hung down below hunched shoulders,
His tail switching, feathery, finely.

Nearing an End

Do you know there are ways
of being cruel to me
you have still left
unexplored?

Are you tired of the game?
Or do you begin, just begin
to want to nurse
my sick love?

I am a man
with a cripple inside him.
He suffers so much I would kill him
if I dared.

Incident

I look across the table and think
(fiery with love)
Ask me, go on, ask me
to do something impossible,
something freakishly useless,
something unimaginable and inimitable

like making a finger break into blossom
or walking for half an hour in twenty minutes
or remembering tomorrow.

I will you to ask it.
But all you say is
Will you give me a cigarette?
And I smile and,
returning to the marvellous world
of possibility,
I give you one
with a hand that trembles
with a human trembling.

July Day Spectacular

I sit in the third row of
gray rocks upholstered
with lichen. Light pours
from the flies of heaven
on a thirty mile stage-set;
and there, by the footlights
of breaking water,
oystercatchers,
going through their old routines,
put on their black-and-white minstrel show
watched by a bandmaster pigeon
with built-in epaulettes.

Bookworm

I open the second volume
of a rose
and find it says, word for word,
the same as the first one.

The waves of the sea
annoy me, they bore me;
why aren't they divided
in paragraphs?

I look at the night
and make nothing of it –
those black pages
with no print.

But I love the gothic script
of pinetrees and
on the pond the light's
fancy italics.

And the cherry tree's petals –
they make
a sweet lyric, I appreciate
their dying fall.

But it's strange, girl, how I come back
from the library of everything
to stare and stare at
the closed book of you.

When will you open to me
and show me the meaning of all
the hard words
in the lexicon of love?

ADRIAN MITCHELL

PHOTOGRAPHS BY FAY GODWIN

Adrian Mitchell was born in London in 1932 and has worked as a journalist. He has written film-scripts; plays; novels; librettos; songs for shows, including *The Hotpot Saga* (a black pantomime about a race war between Lancashire and Yorkshire); *Lash Me To The Mast!* (a musical version of the Odyssey); and *Move Over, Jehovah* or *The Man Who Shot Emily Brontë*, a dramatization of the Old Testament.

His publications include *Poems* (1964), *Out Loud* (1968) and *Ride the Nightmare* (1971). He can be heard reading his poetry on *Poetry and Jazz in Concert* with the Michael Garrick Quintet (Argo DA 26).

Adrian Mitchell's observations for this volume are different from the others' in that they were spoken rather than written. At the time of our conversation he was up to his eyes in rehearsals for the premiere of his play, *Mind Your Head*, in Liverpool.

Adrian Mitchell left his first school because all the younger children were being bullied, and went on to a Wiltshire prep school, where he was very happy. One teacher in particular, Michael Bell, had a very important influence on him; he was a man with a tremendous enthusiasm for drama and literature, who believed in encouraging his pupils in their own creative efforts. In place of the essay assignment in English, Mitchell wrote a play, which the master and other boys produced in secret and performed for him as a surprise. When asked what kind of books he liked reading, he replied that he liked books about imaginary worlds and the master introduced him to *Erewhon* and *Animal Farm*, which he loved. Later, the boys produced a dramatization of Adrian Mitchell's essay *The Animals' Brains Trust* and also put on *Murder in the Cathedral* and *Henry IV part II*, in which Mitchell played the part of Justice Shallow.

Meanwhile, out of school, one of his chief pleasures was going to pantomimes and shows with his mother. His father was more interested in his gardening and scientific interests, which Adrian's brother also shared. When he was ten, he discovered some American comics, in which one of the strips featured Walt Whitman. Mitchell was intrigued by this white-bearded patriarch and spoke of his fascination to his mother, who went out and bought him a very beautiful copy of *Leaves of Grass*. In his early teens, he discovered the war-poems of Siegfried Sassoon and Wilfred Owen and these made an enormous impact on him.

I read Wordsworth in school at an unresponsive time. It tended to be the poetry that I read out of school that I naturally had the loyalty to: Alex Comfort, MacNeice, Kenneth Patchen. I still read them, Dylan Thomas too. I tended to escape from the school room, where we were taking it in turns to read Milton's 'Lycidas' out, and trying

to make each other giggle as we read it. I tended to read contemporary poets when I got outside – those I could get hold of. The American poets were not all that available, so it was a lot later that I discovered William Carlos Williams, who would have delighted me if I'd known his work then.

I hate the way poetry is treated in some schools, but there are primary and secondary schools where the teachers encourage kids to make their own in whatever way they can. I've said to teachers, in moments of desperation, that poetry should be banned in schools: then the kids would really run to it.

I first began to think at all for myself during the first Labour Government, after the war in 1946. Everyone around me was Tory up to that point (except a couple of Liberals), so I thought Churchill was God, like we all did. We all didn't, of course – a lot of people didn't – but I didn't know that at the time. The arguments of the people around me seemed to me to get more and more stupid. I felt there must be some other point of view and thought about it and read something vaguely 'left', and decided I vaguely supported Labour.

Then, at eighteen, I went into the RAF. Up to that point I'd been in private schools. Suddenly, there I was with working-class lads, almost entirely. In the ranks, there was a very rigid class system and I began to understand something about working-class life for the very first time in my life, at the age of eighteen. There were shocking things about it. But I had discovered some shocking things about poverty beforehand. As far as it was a shock, it was a good shock.

I was a teleprinter-operator in the RAF. I was nearly a pacifist, but I wasn't quite sure if I was a pacifist or not. I thought there were some things I would fight about – like concentration camps. I still feel there are some things I'd fight over. I'd never feel good about fighting for something but I feel there are some situations where people are driven to the point where they would kill and in that situation, I would too.

After his national service he went up to Oxford to read English.

I had the special privilege of Oxford. I do think that students at universities are a privileged class because they're a very very small minority and this is one of the difficulties when students say 'We want to get together with the working class'. (I've written about this in the Guardian.) Go into pubs and, wherever you go, you'll find that 'student' is a dirty word, because people think that students are spending three years doing what they want; and some are and some aren't. At least these are three years in which you are not under a boss and not in a job as such. My feeling is that everyone should get three years, to take whenever they want in their lives, and not necessarily for higher education (it would be frightening if everyone chose higher education) in order to go fishing, or exploring – and with a scholarship. It wouldn't be necessary to spend it in an institution, and it wouldn't necessarily be at the age of twenty or after leaving school; but sometime in your life, when you needed it. It wouldn't be just to break down the privilege, although I think that's important, but because I think people deserve more freedom.

Until you have good nursery schools going for everyone who wants them, you won't get anywhere. The creative thing that happens in a good nursery school should go right on up through the system. The emphasis should be on getting people to make things, using what you can get from the past and no holds barred (whether Duke Ellington or Alexander Pope). The emphasis should be towards turning out people who are free from the fear of being creative. The system is not geared at all towards turning out people who create – and I don't just mean Art, but songs, houses, etc.

If the kids have come out of creative nursery schools, it's very important that there should be teachers at the secondary stages (since teachers have the power in this structure) who are going to respond and find out what the kids want. None of us can say beforehand what they are going to want when they have been through that process, because we ourselves did not go through it. I had a bit of it at one point, but kids in future will be increasingly different from what they are now.

At Oxford, he began to write – not essays for his tutor – but student journalism and other things of his own choosing. He left Oxford without taking a degree, and then took a job on the *Oxford Mail*, as a journalist, and from there moved to the *Evening Standard*, where he worked on the *Londoner's Diary* column.

The real confidence didn't come until after I had left Oxford. I knew that I wanted to be a writer by then, but I still didn't know if I could write anything that really satisfied me. After I left, I joined Edward Lucie-Smith's 'The Group'. I went to three meetings of that. At the first one I went to, I read a long poem that I'd written, called 'Veteran with a Head Wound', which is in my first book and which I was very excited about. They liked it a lot and suggested that I have it duplicated and bring it back the next week. In fact, they gave me some very good advice about it. I cut off a stanza which was at the beginning and replaced it by the title. They were very good in their response, which was absolutely what I needed at that time – this was about two years after I had left Oxford – because I was pretty sure that it was a good poem and I still think it is but I did want confirmation and got it. Then I was sure I'd done one, so I could do some more. That gave me tremendous confidence.

I didn't stay on in the group because I wasn't interested in the discussions. I found that all I actually had wanted was just that response to that particular piece of work. It was crucial. If they had all jumped on me and flattened it, I'd have gone on writing, but I'd have had to get a very positive response at some point to be quite as dogged about grabbing time for writing as I have been. I've been very lucky in that, since then, I've always had some friends who have been very supportive in that kind of way.

At about this time his mother died; she left him a small amount of money, and with this he bought his freedom for a year during which he wrote a novel, a libretto and a play. When the money ran out he returned to the *Standard*, and moved into free-lance journalism. In this capacity, he contributed to the pop-column of the *Daily Mail* at about the time the Beatles were bursting onto an unsuspecting world, and also wrote TV criticism.

Peter Brook then asked him to work on the script for the Royal Shakespeare Company's production of *Marat-Sade*, and subsequently he wrote plays both for the theatre and for television. He was also writing poetry, and reading it aloud to a variety of audiences. In the theatre, the major influences on his work have included John Arden and Margaretta D'Arcy, and the work of Albert Hunt in Bradford.

As for his poetry, and the kind of poetry he finds most congenial: My poems should ideally be spoken aloud – or sung. The effect that the audience has on me, when I read them in public, is that, if six different audiences haven't liked a poem, then this might possibly mean that changes to the poem might be made; though not always, depending on what I feel are their reasons for not responding to it.

As for writing a variety of things – novels, plays, poems:
When things are going well, I find myself doing a lot of things at the same time. When things are going badly, it's a question of searching around for what the hell I can do. I prefer to think of myself as a writer whose poems are primarily for performance, and publishing the poems – getting them into print – is in some senses for the benefit of those who heard them being read aloud.

I find reading-tours very exciting, demanding, and exhausting, especially in America. For a poetry-reading, a mixed audience is always the best, with a mixture of ages and sexes: the bigger the mixture the better.

One of the major influences was when I first met Allen Ginsberg, in New York. I did a reading on New Year's morning. Everyone had a hangover, it was snowing and about ten people came. Ginsberg was one of them and he listened, and afterwards we talked. He has a very quick instinct about people, so he talks to you intimately, straight away. He can get what you are on about almost immediately, and he asked me, 'Why don't you write with the rhythms of your speech?'

Many of what seem to be his most important poems have been about public issues, public morality, political morality, about right and wrong. They have a kind of determined categorical quality, as if they're saying: 'This is wrong or this is right; and this seems to me to be very important.'

Yes. It's very important to me. I've used word cartoons in books to describe some of them. If I thought some of them were the equivalent of political cartoons, like R. Cobb, in words, I'd be satisfied.

Ken Sprague, who did the covers of my books The Bodyguard and Ride The Nightmare, is another of my kind of artist. The kind of artist I like tends to have hard edges. The pictures I like are mainly pictures of people, so that Rouault and Blake and Breughel are the people I love best.

As for my political education, it's been pretty patchy. It's got great gaps. A lot of it has been through reading newspapers every day. Of course when I was a journalist, every newspaper, every day. Quite a lot came from working on newspapers and although I wasn't put on political stories, as such, specifically, there hasn't been time to educate myself politically in the way of working through Das Kapital and making up notes and finding a synthesis of all my beliefs. There has never been enough time for reading since university. It's come from lots of things. Someone like John Arden increases my political consciousness. Beckett does as well and also Albert Hunt. From some friends who are a lot more politically aware than I am. From some who are less aware than I am in a theoretical, political sense, but more aware than I am of how to treat other people in that small but essential political way.

What I do does make sense to me. I don't believe we ever reach Utopia. But there is a struggle and things may get better – may get worse – depends on how many people are pushing and how hard. I've got a lot of friends who are working in different ways in the same sort of direction. We give each other energy. Sometimes it's strangers that you get an exchange with.

I haven't written much about my parents – only that one piece – because I haven't wanted to. I think they would have been quite happy about it. I was worried about what my brother would think about it. I didn't want to hurt his feelings at all. He was pleased with it so that was good enough. I couldn't have written it while my parents were alive; it would have embarrassed them, but it was written after they were dead. There are things I wouldn't write because I don't want to hurt people.

If somebody I love starts dropping bombs on somebody, I'll certainly attack them. If somebody I love does something bad in a small way, I shall also attack them but of course in that case I would attack them face to face. There's no need to go into print to do that. If they do things in a big public way – something very bad – I might find it necessary to attack them in print.

There are certain alliances, of course. In all alliances there comes a point where they may have to be broken if somebody does something which you feel absolutely opposed to, as distinct from something you'd sooner they hadn't done, but which isn't absolutely against what you feel you stand for.

When people say categorically: 'When I write poems, I don't think of anyone reading them' I don't believe that totally. There are certain place-names which I could put in a poem and immediately to me those place-names might conjure up joy or terror, but I know it wouldn't for anyone else, so I can't just use that name unless I explain. I can use it for a title perhaps and then the poem shows what I feel about it. There is a kind of code which can't be cracked and a kind of obscurity which I don't want because I want to talk as clearly as possible. Every poet wants to talk as clearly as possible. Some people would be talking about complicated visions, because that's what they get, so their poetry is more complicated; and some may be more intellectual and be more concerned with the classics and may assume a classical audience. I don't have a classical background and my heroes tend to be more commonly held. (I want to write a series of poems about Duke Ellington and about Ellington's band.) Someone like Ellington or Charlie Parker or other people who wend in and out of my poems, they just happen to be better known. It's not a conscious choice – I have written about Aeschylus!

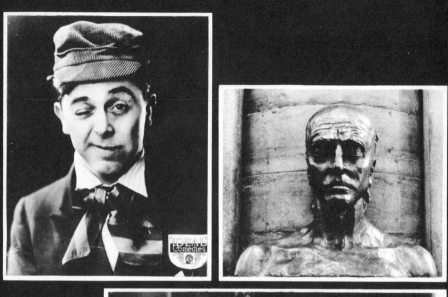

My Parents

My father died the other day and I would like to write about him. Because I think of them together, this means also writing about my mother, who died several years ago.

About a thousand people called her Kay, most of them people she helped at some time, for she was what chintzy villains call a 'do-gooder'. Nobody ever called her that to her face or in my family's hearing; if they had, she'd have felt sorry for them. Both her brothers were killed in the First World War. She divided her life between loving her family, bullying or laughing innumerable committees into action rather than talk, giving, plotting happiness for other people, and keeping up an exuberant correspondence with several hundred friends.

She was not afraid of anyone. She was right. A Fabian near-pacifist, she encouraged me to argue, assuming right-wing positions sometimes so that I was forced to fight and win the discussion.

She tried to hoist the whole world on her shoulders. After each of her first two cancer operations, on her breasts, she seemed to clench her fists and double the energy with which she gave. She wasn't interested in unshared pleasure.

After the second operation she answered the door one day to a poor woman whom she didn't know. The woman asked where 'the wise woman' lived. My mother knew whom she meant – a rich clairvoyant who lived down the road. Not trusting that particular witch, my mother asked what was wrong. The poor woman's doctor had told her that she must have a breast removed, and she was very scared. My mother said, but there's nothing to that, look – and she took out the two rolled socks which she kept in her empty brassiere and threw them up into the sunlight and then caught them again. So the poor woman came in, drank tea, talked, forgot many fears, and went away knowing that she had seen the wise woman.

People called my father Jock. Face tanned from working in his garden, he survived the trenches of the First World War. He spoke very little. When he talked it was either very funny or very important. He only spoke to me about his war twice, and then briefly. In my teens I wrote a short, Owen-influenced poem about the war. My father read it, then told me of a friend who, during the lull between bombardments, fell to all fours and howled like an animal and was never cured.

Usually he avoided company. There was something in other people which frightened him. He was right. At the seaside he would sit on the farthest-out rock and fish peacefully. When visitors called at our house he would generally disappear into his jungle of raspberry canes and lurk.

Maybe there were twenty or thirty people in the world whose company he really enjoyed. They were lucky; he was a lovely man. Like

Edward Lear, he was most at his ease with children, who instantly read, in the lines radiating from the corners of his eyes, that this was a man who understood their games and jokes.

After my mother's death, he was a desolated man. But when he remarried, very happily, light came back into his face and he learned to smile again. He was short and lean and had fantastic sprouting Scottish eyebrows. He was a research chemist, but that didn't mean he only took an interest and pride in my elder brother's scientific work. He let me see how glad he was that I wrote, and I still remember the stories he used to write for me and my brother.

A year or so before he died he was in London for the day. My father sometimes voted Tory, sometimes Liberal, but when he began to talk about Vietnam that day, his face became first red and then white with anger about the cruelty and stupidity of the war. I seldom saw him angry and never so angry as at that moment, a man of seventy, not much interested in politics, all the grief of 1914–18 marching back into his mind.

People sometimes talk as if the ideological conflicts between generations have to be fought out bloodily, as if it is inevitable that children should grow to hate their parents. I don't believe this. Our family was lucky: my brother and I were always free to choose for ourselves – knowing that, however odd our decisions, we were trusted and loved. We all loved one another and this love was never shadowed.

Time and Motion Study

Slow down the film. You see that bit.
Seven days old and no work done.
Two hands clutching nothing but air,
Two legs kicking nothing but air.
That yell. There's wasted energy there.
No use to himself, no good for the firm.
Make a note of that.

New film. Now look, now he's fourteen.
Work out the energy required
To make him grow that tall.
It could have been used
It could have all been used
For the good of the firm and he could have stayed small.
Make a note of that.

Age thirty. And the waste continues.
Using his legs for walking. Tiring
His mouth with talking and eating. Twitching.
Slow it down. Reproducing? I see.
All, I suppose, for the good of the firm.
But he'd better change methods. Yes, he'd better.
Look at the waste of time and emotion,
Look at the waste. Look. Look.
And make a note of that.

Night Lines in a Peaceful Farmhouse

truth is
exactly the same size as the universe
and my eyes are narrow

i stare at one of my fingernails
its mass is pink
its edge is blue with coke dust
it grows on a warm well-nourished hand

i look up and suck smoke
the windows are black

people are being killed

the first time i met a girl called Helen
she told me
'money is the basis of life'
the second time i met her she said
'money is the basis of life'

people are being killed

i stare at those four words
typed in black
they are true words
but they do not bleed
and die and rot

commonplace cruelty
timetable cruelty

i haven't seen much of the world
but i've seen enough

i have known more horror in half an hour
than i shall ever have the skill to tell

my right hand soothes my left hand

i have known more beauty in half a minute
than i shall ever have the skill to tell

i make a fond small smile
remembering gentleness in many cities

so many good people

and people are being killed

The Castaways or **Vote for Caliban**

The Pacific Ocean –
A blue demi-globe.
Islands like punctuation marks.

A cruising airliner.
Passengers unwrapping pats of butter.
A hurricane arises
And tosses the plane into the sea.

Five of them, flung on to an island beach,
Survived.
Tom the reporter.
Susan the botanist.
Jim the high jump champion.
Bill the carpenter.
Mary the eccentric widow.

Tom the reporter sniffed out a stream of drinkable water.
Susan the botanist identified a banana tree.
Jim the high jump champion jumped up and down and gave them
each a bunch.
Bill the carpenter knocked up a table for their banana supper.
Mary the eccentric widow buried the banana skins,
But only after they had asked her twice.
They all gathered sticks and lit a fire.
There was an incredible sunset.

Next morning they held a committee meeting.
Tom, Susan, Jim and Bill
Voted to make the best of things.
Mary, the eccentric widow, abstained.

Tom the reporter killed several dozen wild pigs.
He tanned their skins into parchment
And printed the *Island News* with the ink of squids.

Susan the botanist developed new strains of banana
Which tasted of chocolate, beefsteak, peanut butter,
Chicken and bootpolish.

Jim the high jump champion organized organized games
Which he always won easily.

Bill the carpenter constructed a wooden water wheel
And converted the water's energy into electricity.
Using iron ore from the hills, he constructed lampposts.

They all worried about Mary the eccentric widow,
Her lack of confidence and her –
But there wasn't time to coddle her.

The volcano erupted, but they dug a trench
And diverted the lava into the sea
Where it formed a spectacular pier.
They were attacked by pirates but defeated them
With bamboo bazookas firing
Sea-urchins packed with home-made nitro-glycerine.
They gave the cannibals a dose of their own medicine
And survived an earthquake thanks to their skill in jumping.

They were resourceful, they were plucky
And by general agreement they abstained from sex.

Tom had been a court reporter
So he became the magistrate and solved disputes.
Susan the Botanist established
A University which also served as a Museum.
Jim the high jump champion
Was put in charge of law-enforcement,
Jumped on them when they were bad.
Bill the carpenter built himself a church,
Preached there every Sunday.

But Mary the eccentric widow . . .
Each evening she wandered down the island's main street.
Past the Stock Exchange, the Houses of Parliament,
The prison and the arsenal.
Past the Prospero Souvenir Shop,
Past the Robert Louis Stevenson Movie Studios,
Past the Daniel Defoe Motel
She nervously wandered and sat on the pier of lava,
Breathing heavily,
As if at a loss,
As if at a lover,
She opened her eyes wide
To the usual incredible sunset.

Veteran with a Head Wound

Nothing to show for it at first
But dreams and shivering, a few mistakes.
Shapes lounged around his mind chatting of murder,
Telling interminable jokes,
Watching like tourists for Vesuvius to burst.

He started listening. Too engrossed to think,
He let his body move in jerks,
Talked just to prove himself alive, grew thin,
Lost five jobs in eleven weeks,
Then started drinking, blamed it on the drink.

He'd seen a woman, belly tattered, run
Her last yards. He had seen a fat
Friend roll in flames, as if his blood were paraffin,
And herded enemies waiting to be shot
Stand looking straight into the sun.

They couldn't let him rot in the heat
In the corner of England like a garden chair.
A handy-man will take a weathered chair,
Smooth it, lay on a glowing layer
Of paint and tie a cushion to the seat.

They did all anyone could do –
Tried to grate off the colour of his trouble,
Brighten him up a bit. His rare
Visitors found him still uncomfortable.
The old crimson paint showed through.

Each night he heard from the back of his head,
As he was learning to sleep again,
Funny or terrible voices tell
Or ask him how their deaths began.
These are the broadcasts of the dead.

One voice became a plaintive bore.
It could only remember the grain and shine
Of a wooden floor, the forest smell
Of its fine surface. The voice rasped on
For hours about that pretty floor.

'If I could make that floor again,'
The voice insisted, over and over,
'The floor on which I died,' it said,
'Then I could stand on it for ever
Letting the scent of polish lap my brain.'

He became Boswell to the dead.
In cruel script their deaths are written.
Generously they are fed
In that compound for the forgotten,
His crowded, welcoming head.

The doctors had seen grimmer cases.
They found his eyes were one-way mirrors,
So they could easily look in
While he could only see his terrors,
Reflections of those shuttered faces.

Stepping as far back as I dare,
(For the man may stagger and be broken
Like a bombed factory or hospital),
I see his uniform is woven
Of blood, bone, flesh and hair.

Populated by the simple dead,
This soldier, in his happy dreams,
Is killed before he kills at all.
Bad tenant that he is, I give him room;
He is the weeper in my head.

Since London's next bomb will tear
Her body in its final rape,
New York and Moscow's ashes look the same
And Europe go down like a battleship,
Why should one soldier make me care?

Ignore him or grant him a moment's sadness.
He walks the burning tarmac road
To the asylum built with bricks of flame.
Abandon him and you must make your own
House of incinerating madness.

The horizon is only paces away.
We walk an alley through a dark,
Criminal city. None can pass.
We would have to make love, fight or speak
If we met someone travelling the other way.

A tree finds its proportions without aid.
Dogs are not tutored to be fond.
Penny-size frogs traverse the grass
To the civilization of a pond.
Grass withers yearly, is re-made.

Trees become crosses because man is born.
Dogs may be taught to shrink from any hand.
Dead frogs instruct the scientist;
Spread clouds of poison in the pond –
You kill their floating globes of spawn.

In London, where the trees are lean,
The banners of the grass are raised.
Grass feeds the butcher and the beast,
But we could conjure down a blaze
Would scour the world of the colour green.

For look, though the human soil is tough,
Our state scratches itself in bed
And a thousand are pierced by its fingernails.
It combs its hair, a thousand good and bad
Fall away like discs of dandruff.

For a moment it closes its careful fist
And, keening for the world of streets,
More sons of God whisper in jails
Where the unloved the unloved meet.
The days close round them like a dirty mist.

When death covers England with a sheet
Of red and silver fire, who'll mourn the state,
Though some will live and some bear children
And some of the children born in hate
May be both lovely and complete?

Try to distract this soldier's mind
From his distraction. Under the powdered buildings
He lies alive, still shouting,
With his brothers and sisters and perhaps his children,
While we bury all the dead people we can find.

Open Day at Porton

These bottles are being filled with madness,
A kind of liquid madness concentrate
Which can be drooled across the land
Leaving behind a shuddering human highway . . .

A welder trying to eat his arm.

Children pushing stale food into their eyes
To try to stop the chemical spectaculars
Pulsating inside their hardening skulls.

A health visitor throwing herself downstairs,
Climbing the stairs, throwing herself down again
Shouting: Take the nails out of my head.

There is no damage to property.

Now, nobody likes manufacturing madness,
But if we didn't make madness in bottles
We wouldn't know how to deal with bottled madness.

We don't know how to deal with bottled madness.

We all really hate manufacturing madness
But if we didn't make madness in bottles
We wouldn't know how to be sane.

Responsible madness experts assure us
Britain would never be the first
To uncork such a global brainquake.

But suppose some foreign nut sprayed Kent
With his insanity aerosol . . .
Well, there's only one answer to madness.

Under Photographs of Two Party Leaders, Smiling

These two smiled so the photographer
Could record their smiles
    FOR YOU

As they smiled these smiles
They were thinking all the time
    OF YOU

They smile on the rich
They smile on the poor
They smile on the victim in his village
They smile on the killer in his cockpit

    Yes, Mummy and Daddy
    Are smiling, smiling
    AT YOU

    please try to smile back.

ROYAL POEMS

The *Daily Telegraph* wrote asking me: 'Could you, for instance, let us have some verse on how you see the relationship that exists between the Prince of Wales and the Welsh people? Obviously it is quite impossible for us to let you have a clear brief, but what we hope to achieve is something that will in some way reflect the Welsh mood as we see it, or even as they see it.' I responded by return of post with the following:

To Charles Windsor-Mountbatten

Royalty is a neurosis.
    Get well soon.

The *Daily Telegraph* rejected my contribution politely, but they'd started something and, after a week's research in which I established beyond reasonable doubt my claim to the throne of England, I wrote a series of regal bits in my new persona as the Rightful King of England.

Loyal Ode to Myself on My Installation as Prince of Yorkshire

Applauded by the loyal West Riding drizzle
I progressed up the A65
Bearing the symbol of my temporal power,
An iced lolly, very cold and powerfully purple.
Under my purple breath
I swore eternal fealty to myself
Against all manner of folks.
Nobody threw any eggs at ME.

Decree to all Members of the Church of England

We, His Majesty, the Rightful King of England,
Do hereby publish and decree
And do most hideously command on pain of pain
That all baptized members of our Church of England
Shall sell all that they have
And bring the wherewithal therefrom
To our most Royal Treasury.
We shall await your loyal tributes
At the summit of Primrose Hill
At noon on October 24th this year,
Cash please, no cheques.
Yours sincerely,
Defender of the Faith.

The Royal Prerogative of Mercy

Put that woman down at once!
We know she's upset you,
We know she's got a face
Like a breach of the peace,
But give her back her horse,
Return her knickers.
We are a merciful King
Even to women in military uniform
Who pretend to be the Queen of England.

Final Chant
(from *The Body*)

Long live the child
Long live the mother and father
Long live man

Long live this wounded planet
Long live the good milk of the air
Long live the spawning rivers and the mothering oceans
Long live the juice of the grass
and all the determined greenery of the globe
Long live the surviving animals
Long live the earth, deeper than all our thinking

We have done enough killing

Long live the man
Long live the woman
Who use both courage and compassion
Long live their children

Solid Citizens

Let us praise the dead

Snug in their wooden homes
Under the aerials of Christ
Keeping themselves to themselves.

They do not strike or demonstrate;

Should they do so
They would lose the support
Of a sympathetic public.

Divide and Rule for as Long as You Can

Glasgow.
Trade Unionists march through the Square
Towards the City Chambers.

Police. Police. Police.

And in the streets leading off the square –
Scottish soldiers with rifles.
Live ammunition.
They may be ordered to shoot into the crowd.

And behind the Scottish soldiers –
English soldiers with rifles.
Live ammunition.
If the Scottish soldiers refuse to shoot into the crowd
The English soldiers will be ordered
To shoot the Scottish soldiers.

Oh, but that was long ago.

That was in the future.

Briefing

He may be fanatical, he may have a madness.
Either way, move carefully.
He must be surrounded, but he's contagious.

One of you will befriend his family.
One male and one female will love the subject
Until he loves you back. Gradually

Our team will abstract and collect
His mail, nail-clippings, garbage, friends, words, schemes,
Graphs of his fears, scars, sex and intellect.

Steam open his heart. Tap his dreams.
Learn him inside and inside out.
When he laughs, laugh. Scream when he screams.

He will scream. 'Innocent!' He'll shout
Until his mouth is broken with stones.
We use stones. We take him out

To a valley full of stones.
He stands against a shed. He stands on stones
Naked. The initial stones

Shower the iron shed. Those stones
Outline the subject. When he cries for stones
The clanging ceases. Then we give him stones,

Filling his universe with stones.
Stones – his atoms turn to stones
And he becomes a stone buried in stones.

A final tip. Then you may go.
Note the half-hearted stoners and watch how
Your own arm throws. And watch how I throw.

Cease-Fire
(dedicated to the work of Medical Aid for Vietnam,
36 Wellington Street, London WC2)

The outside of my body was half-eaten
by the fire which clings as tight as skin.
The fire has turned some of my skin
into black scab bits of roughness
and some pale bits, smooth as plastic,
which no one dares touch
except me and the doctor.

Everyone who looks at me is scared.
That's not because I want to hurt people
but because so much of me
looks like the meat of a monster.

I was walking to the market.
Then I was screaming.
They found me screaming.
They put out the flames on my skin.
They laid me on a stretcher and I cried:
Not on my back!
So they turned me over and I cried:
Not on my front!

A doctor put a needle in my arm
And my mind melted
and I fell into a furnace of dreams of furnaces.

When I woke up I was in a white hospital.
Everything I wanted to say scared me
and I did not want to scare the others
in that white hospital,
so I said nothing, I cried as quietly as I could.

Months passed over my head
and bombers passed over my head
and people came and said they were my parents
and they found out the right places on my face
where I could bear to be kissed.

And I pretended I could see them
but I couldn't really look out of my eyes
but only inwards, into my head
where the flames still clung and hurt.

And the voice of the flames said:
You are meat.
You are most ugly meat.
Your body cannot grow to loveliness.
Nobody could love such ugly meat.
Only ugly meat could love such ugly meat.
Better be stewed for soup and eaten.

And months passed over my head
and the bombers passed over my head
and the voices of the flames began to flicker
and I began to believe
the people who said they were my parents
were my parents.

And one day I threw myself forward
so that I sat up in bed, for the first time,
and hurled my arms around my mother,
and however the skin of my chest howled out its pain
I held her, I held her, I held her
and knew she was my mother.
And I forgot that I was monster meat
and I knew she did not know that I was monster meat.

I held her, I held her.

And, sweet sun which blesses all the world –
all the flames faded.
The flames of my skin
and the flames inside my head –
all the flames faded
and I was flooded
with love for my mother
who did not know
that I was monster meat.

And so, in the love-flood, I let go of my mother
and fell back upon my pillow
and I rolled my head to the left side
and saw a child, or it might have been an old man,
eating his rice with his only arm
and I rolled my head to the right side
and saw another child, or she might have been an old woman,
being fed through the arm from a tube from a red bottle –
and I loved them, and, flooded with love
I started to sing
the song of the game I used to play with my friends
in the long-ago days before the flames came:

> One, one, I bounce the ball.
> Once for the cobbler at the corner.
> Two, two, I bounce the ball.
> Twice for the fisherman on the river.
> Three, three, I bounce the ball.
> Three times for my golden lover –

And had to stop singing.
Throat choked with vomit.

And then the flames exploded again all over my skin
and then the flames exploded again inside my head
and I burned, sweet sun, sweet mother, I burned.

Sweet sun, which blesses all the world,
this was one of the people of Vietnam.
Make him or her whatever age you like –
he or she is dead.

The one-armed man or boy survives.
The woman or girl
whose body needs a change of blood each day
survives.

I suppose we love each other.
We're stupid if we don't.

We have a choice –
Either to choke to death on our own vomit
or to become one
with the sweet sun, which blesses all the world.

Norman Morrison

On November 2nd 1965
in the multi-coloured multi-minded
United beautiful States of terrible America
Norman Morrison set himself on fire
outside the Pentagon.
He was thirty-one, he was a Quaker,
and his wife (seen weeping in the newsreels)
and his three children
survive him as best they can.
He did it in Washington where everyone could see
because
people were being set on fire
in the dark corners of Vietnam where nobody could see.
Their names, ages, beliefs and loves
are not recorded.
This is what Norman Morrison did.
He poured petrol over himself.
He burned. He suffered.
He died.
That is what he did
in the white heat of Washington
where everyone could see.
He simply burned away his clothes,
his passport, his pink-tinted skin,
put on a new skin of flame
and became
Vietnamese.

Hear the Voice of the Critic

There are too many colours.
The Union Jack's all right, selective,
Two basic colours and one negative,
Reasonable, avoids confusion.
      (Of course I respect the red, white and blue)

But there are too many colours.
The rainbow, well it's gaudy, but I am
Bound to admit, a useful diagram
When treated as an optical illusion.
      (Now I'm not saying anything against rainbows)

But there are too many colours.
Take the sea. Unclassifiable.
The sky – the worst offender of all,
Tasteless as Shakespeare, especially at sunset.
      (I wish my body were all one colour).

There are too many colours.
I collect flat white plates.
You ought to see my flat white plates.
In my flat white flat I have a perfect set,
      (It takes up seven rooms).

There are too many colours.

Leaflets
(for Brian Patten and my twelve students at Bradford)

Outside the plasma supermarket
I stretch out my arm to the shoppers and say:
'Can I give you one of these?'

I give each of them a leaf from a tree.

The first shopper thanks me.
The second puts the leaf in his mack pocket where his wife won't see.
The third says she is not interested in leaves. She looks like a mutilated
    willow.
The fourth says: 'Is it art?' I say that it is a leaf.
The fifth looks through his leaf and smiles at the light beyond.
The sixth hurls down his leaf and stamps it till dark purple mud oozes
    through.
The seventh says she will press it in her album.
The eighth complains that it is an oak leaf and says he would be on my
    side if I were also handing out birch leaves, apple leaves, privet
    leaves and larch leaves. I say that it is a leaf.
The ninth takes the leaf carefully and then, with a backhand fling,
    gives it its freedom.
It glides, following surprise curving alleys through the air.
It lands. I pick it up.
The tenth reads both sides of the leaf twice and then says: 'Yes, but it
    doesn't say who we should kill.'

But you took your leaf like a kiss.

They tell me that, on Saturdays,
You can be seen in your own city centre
Giving away forests, orchards, jungles.

The Marie Lloyd Song
(from the play *Mind Your Head*. To be sung to the
Welsh hymn-tune, Calon Lan)

Marie Lloyd was warm as kettles
And as frank as celluloid
And her words could sting like nettles
Or caress like Marie Lloyd

Marie Lloyd come back and warm us
Marie Lloyd return to us
For your heart was as enormous
As a double-decker bus

Like a farted interruption
Of a speech by Sigmund Freud
Like Mount Etna in eruption
Is the heart of Marie Lloyd

Marie Lloyd come back and warm us
Marie Lloyd return to us
For your heart is as enormous
As a double-decker bus

She had eyes like Dylan Thomas
And the wit of Nye Bevan
Marie Lloyd was taken from us
Send her back to succour man

Marie Lloyd come back and warm us
Marie Lloyd return to us
For your heart is as enormous
As a double-decker bus

Bessie Smith in Yorkshire

As I looked over the billowing West Riding
A giant golden tractor tumbled over the horizon
The grass grew blue and the limestone changed to meat
For Bessie Smith was bumping in the driver's seat

Threw myself down on the fertilized ground and cried:
'When I was a foetus I loved you, and I love you now you've died.'
She was bleeding beauty from her wounds in the Lands of Wrong
But she kept on travelling and she spent all her breathing on song

I was malleted into the earth as tight as a gate-post
She carried so much life I felt like the ghost of a ghost
She's the river that runs straight uphill
Hers is the voice brings my brain to a standstill

Black tracking wheels
Roll around the planet
Seeds of the blues
Bust through the concrete

My pale feet fumble along
The footpaths of her midnight empire

A Good Idea

It should be the kind which stiffens and grows a skin
But the creamier kind will do.
Anyway, the Royal Albert Hall must be filled with custard.

Early Shift on the *Evening Standard* News Desk

Fog Chaos Grips South

A thick blanket of fog lay across Southern England this morning
like a thick blanket –

'Don't let's call it a thick blanket today Joe, let's call it a
sodden yellow eiderdown.'

'Are you insane?'

Incident

At Chorley Station on May 30th, 1969, I saw a railwayman
bailing out the signal-box with a pewter mug and pouring
the water inaccurately down into a scarlet wheelbarrow.

Goodbye

He breathed in air, he breathed out light.
Charlie Parker was my delight.

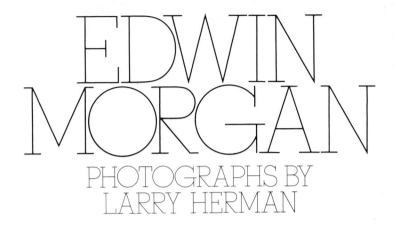

EDWIN MORGAN

PHOTOGRAPHS BY LARRY HERMAN

Edwin Morgan was born in 1920, and was educated at Glasgow University, where he now teaches. His work as a translator includes texts from French, Italian and Russian, as well as Anglo-Saxon. His recreations include colour photography, scrapbooks and looking at cities.

His publications include *The Second Life* (1968), *From Glasgow to Saturn* (1973), *Twelve Songs*, *The Horseman's Word*, *Glasgow Sonnets*, *Instamatic Poems*; a translation of *Beowulf*; a translation into Lallans of the poems of Mayakovsky, *Wi the Haill Voice*; and *Poems from Eugenio Montale*. He has also edited, with George Bruce and Maurice Lindsay, *Scottish Poetry*, vols. I–VI, published by the Edinburgh University Press.

There is a poetry before poetry – that is what I seem to see if I look back to my boyhood. Ours was not a particularly bookish house, and neither of my parents was interested in poetry or the other arts, though my father had been a great theatregoer in his youth, and kept the cast-lists from old programmes pasted in an album. Nor did any poetry I learned at school leave a very strong impression until my last two years, when Keats and Tennyson suddenly took hold of me. (Modern poetry was not taught at all. I got as far as Bridges and Brooke.) But the imagination of someone who is going to write poetry can be stirred in all sorts of preparatory ways – through popular songs, through nature, through prose, through visual images, through knowledge. In this context, there are things I remember most vividly: my uncle Frank, who had a good tenor voice, sitting at the piano to sing 'Pale hands I love beside the Shalimar' or 'Ramona' or 'Charmain', the strange longing filtering out over playing-cards, bobbed heads and cigarette-smoke; my father (who worked for a firm of iron and steel scrap merchants) describing on a long Sunday walk how steel was made, the whole process – lurid, fearsome, yet controlled, an image of power and danger – coming alive in my mind simply through the evocative force of words; looking again and again through a Victorian volume of my grandmother's filled with engravings of storms, wrecks and exotic atolls and icebergs, and stories of maritime adventure and endurance; poring with a torch under the bedclothes over sets of cigarette-cards like 'Romance of the Heavens' and being equally fascinated by the 'romance' and the scientific facts; discovering, on a family holiday at North Berwick, that the newly intense feelings I was having about sea and sun, and fields of poppies, and the passing of time and the seasons, were going to give me no rest or satisfaction until I had put them into my own words, sometimes in essays, sometimes in letters, sometimes in verse. At that time, while I was still at school, I was writing more prose than poetry, and took great pleasure in creating huge fantastic narratives which probably reflected my liking for Verne, Wells and Edgar Rice Burroughs. It may be that more of my 'poetry' was channelled into prose tales and imaginative essays (on both of which I spent much time and energy) than into verse, though I was also beginning to explore verse expression; and this may be linked with the fact that I knew almost nothing of modern poetry till I went to university at the age of seventeen. Then I read Eliot in English, Rimbaud in French, and Mayakovsky in Russian, and a whole world, or series of worlds, of which I had not had the remotest inkling, began to explode in my mind as the novas on the cigarette-cards had done, in their own way, years before.

I think of poetry as partly an instrument of exploration, like a spaceship, into new fields of feeling or experience (or old fields which become new in new contexts or environments), and partly a special way of recording moments and events (taking the 'prose' of them, the grit of the facts of the case, as being in our age extremely important). I don't find myself relating what I do to other poetry to any great extent. I have had a long and hard search, through my own writing rather than through any conscious apprenticeships to other poets, to find a voice that I could call mine.

It would be wrong not to acknowledge the liberating effect of the American non-academic poets I read in the late 1950s (the Beats led me on to Black Mountain, Williams, Creeley), and then of the Brazilian concrete poets I discovered in 1962. I am also aware of a deep, almost spooky underground debt to some poetry in the Scotch tradition (certain aspects of Dunbar and Burns). And I have learned much from translating foreign poets (Montale and Mayakovsky in particular). But I like a poetry that comes not out of 'poetry' but out of a story in today's newspaper, or a chance personal encounter in a city street, or the death of a famous person: I am very strongly moved by the absolute force of what actually happens, because after all, that is it, there is really nothing else that has its poignance, its razor edge. It is not an easy poetry to write, and I think it requires a peculiar kind of imagination that is willing to bend itself to meet a world which is lying there in the rain like an old shoe.

Maybe it is for the same reason that my concrete poems have titles and are 'about' something. If the element of wit is to succeed in such poems, reality must be around and must be able to be appealed to. In the concrete poems, it is the strange mixture of a strict structural idea and verbal play that I find exhilarating – not so strange perhaps in the end, since 'play' is only within limits 'free' and usually implies a 'game' which of necessity has its own rules. Only in poetry the game cannot be played twice, and the element of exploration is always there, whether of form or of experience.

Trio

Coming up Buchanan Street, quickly, on a sharp winter evening
a young man and two girls, under the Christmas lights –
The young man carries a new guitar in his arms,
the girl on the inside carries a very young baby,
and the girl on the outside carries a chihuahua.
And the three of them are laughing, their breath rises
in a cloud of happiness, and as they pass
the boy says, 'Wait till he sees this but!'
The chihuahua has a tiny Royal Stewart tartan coat like a teapot-
　　holder,
the baby in its white shawl is all bright eyes and mouth like favours
　　in a fresh sweet cake,
the guitar swells out under its milky plastic cover, tied at the neck
　　with silver tinsel tape and a brisk sprig of mistletoe.
Orphean sprig! Melting baby! Warm chihuahua!
The vale of tears is powerless before you.
Whether Christ is born, or is not born, you
put paid to fate, it abdicates
　　　　　　　　　　　　under the Christmas lights.
Monsters of the year
go blank, are scattered back,
can't bear this march of three.

– And the three have passed, vanished in the crowd
(yet not vanished, for in their arms they wind
the life of men and beasts, and music,
laughter ringing them round like a guard)
at the end of this winter's day.

The Suspect

Asked me for a match suddenly/with his hand up
I thought he was after my wallet
gave him a shove/he fell down
dead on the pavement at my feet
he was forty-two, a respectable man they said
anyone can have a bad heart I told the police
but they've held me five hours and don't
tell me the innocent don't feel
guilty in the glaring chair

I didn't kill you/I didn't know you
I did push you/I did fear you
accusing me from the mortuary drawer
like a damned white ghost I don't believe in
– then why were you afraid/are you used to attacks
by men who want a match/what sort
of life you lead/you were bloody quick
with your hands when you pushed him
what did you think he was and do you think
we don't know what you are/take it
all down/the sweat of the innocent by god we'll see
and not by the hundred-watt bulb of the anglepoise either
give him a clip on the ear jack/you
bastard in your shroud if I feared you then
I hate you now you
no I don't you poor dead man I put you there
I don't I don't
but just

if you could get up/to speak for me
I am on trial/do you understand
I am not guilty/whatever the light says
whatever the sweat says
/they've noticed my old scar
to be killed by a dead man is no fight
they're starting again
so/your story is he asked you for a light
– yes suddenly/and put his hand up/I thought
he was after my wallet, gave him
a shove, he fell as I told you
dead, it was his heart,
at my feet, as I said

Glasgow Green

Clammy midnight, moonless mist.
A cigarette glows and fades on a cough.
Meth-men mutter on benches,
pawed by river fog. Monteith Row
sweats coldly, crumbles, dies
slowly. All shadows are alive.
Somewhere a shout's forced out – 'No!' –
it leads to nothing but silence,
except the whisper of the grass
and the other whispers that fill the shadows.

'What d'ye mean see me again?
D'ye think I came here jist for that?
I'm no finished with you yet.
I can get the boys t'ye, they're no that faur away.
You wouldny like that eh? Look there's no two ways aboot it.
Christ but I'm gaun to have you Mac
if it takes all night, turn over you bastard
turn over, I'll ——'
                    Cut the scene.
Here there's no crying for help,
it must be acted out, again, again.
This is not the delicate nightmare
you carry to the point of fear
and wake from, it is life, the sweat
is real, the wrestling under a bush
is real, the dirty starless river
is the real Clyde, with a dishrag dawn
it rinses the horrors of the night
but cannot make them clean,
though washing blows
                    where the women watch
by day,
        and children run,
                    on Glasgow Green.

And how shall these men live?
Providence, watch them go!
Watch them love, and watch them die!
How shall the race be served?
It shall be served by anguish
as well as by children at play.
It shall be served by loneliness
as well as by family love.

It shall be served by hunter and hunted in their endless chain
as well as by those who turn back the sheets in peace.
The thorn in the flesh!
Providence, water it!
Do you think it is not watered?
Do you think it is not planted?
Do you think there is not a seed of the thorn
as there is also a harvest of the thorn?
Man, take in that harvest!
Help that tree to bear its fruit!
Water the wilderness, walk there, reclaim it!
Reclaim, regain, renew! Fill the barns and the vats!

Longing,
            longing
                        shall find its wine.

Let the women sit in the Green
and rock their prams as the sheets
blow and whip in the sunlight.
But the beds of married love
are islands in a sea of desire.
Its waves break here, in this park,
splashing the flesh as it trembles
like driftwood through the dark.

In the Snack-Bar

A cup capsizes along the formica,
slithering with a dull clatter.
A few heads turn in the crowded evening snack-bar.
An old man is trying to get to his feet
from the low round stool fixed to the floor.
Slowly he levers himself up, his hands have no power.
He is up as far as he can get. The dismal hump
looming over him forces his head down.
He stands in his stained beltless gaberdine
like a monstrous animal caught in a tent
in some story. He sways slightly,
the face not seen, bent down
in shadow under his cap.
Even on his feet he is staring at the floor
or would be, if he could see.

I notice now his stick, once painted white
but scuffed and muddy, hanging from his right arm.
Long blind, hunchback born, half paralysed
he stands
fumbling with the stick
and speaks:
'I want – to go to the – toilet.'

It is down two flights of stairs, but we go.
I take his arm. 'Give me – your arm – it's better,' he says.
Inch by inch we drift towards the stairs.
A few yards of floor are like a landscape
to be negotiated, in the slow setting out
time has almost stopped. I concentrate
my life to his: crunch of spilt sugar,
tidy puddle from the night's umbrellas,
table edges, people's feet,
hiss of the coffee-machine, voices and laughter,
smell of a cigar, hamburgers, wet coats steaming,
and the slow dangerous inches to the stairs.
I put his right hand on the rail
and take his stick. He clings to me. The stick
is in his left hand, probing the treads.
I guide his arm and tell him the steps.
And slowly we go down. And slowly we go down.
White tiles and mirrors at last. He shambles
uncouth into the clinical gleam.
I set him in position, stand behind him
and wait with his stick.
His brooding reflection darkens the mirror
but the trickle of his water is thin and slow,
an old man's apology for living.
Painful ages to close his trousers and coat –
I do up the last buttons for him.
He asks doubtfully, 'Can I – wash my hands?'
I fill the basin, clasp his soft fingers round the soap.
He washes, feebly, patiently. There is no towel.
I press the pedal of the drier, draw his hands
gently into the roar of the hot air.
But he cannot rub them together,
drags out a handkerchief to finish.
He is glad to leave the contraption, and face the stairs.
He climbs, and steadily enough.
He climbs, we climb. He climbs
with many pauses but with that one

persisting patience of the undefeated
which is the nature of man when all is said.
And slowly we go up. And slowly we go up.
The faltering, unfaltering steps
take him at last to the door
across that endless, yet not endless waste of floor.
I watch him helped on a bus. It shudders off in the rain.
The conductor bends to hear where he wants to go.

Wherever he could go it would be dark
and yet he must trust men.
Without embarrassment or shame
he must announce his most pitiful needs
in a public place. No one sees his face.
Does he know how frightening he is in his strangeness
under his mountainous coat, his hands like wet leaves
stuck to the half-white stick?
His life depends on many who would evade him.
But he cannot reckon up the chances,
having one thing to do,
to haul his blind hump through these rains of August.
Dear Christ, to be born for this!

One Cigarette

No smoke without you, my fire.
After you left,
your cigarette glowed on in my ashtray
and sent up a long thread of such quiet grey
I smiled to wonder who would believe its signal
of so much love. One cigarette
in the non-smoker's tray.
As the last spire
trembles up, a sudden draught
blows it winding into my face.
Is it smell, is it taste?
You are here again, and I am drunk on your tobacco lips.
Out with the light.
Let the smoke lie back in the dark.
Till I hear the very ash
sigh down among the flowers of brass
I'll breathe, and long past midnight, your last kiss.

The Death of Marilyn Monroe

What innocence? Whose guilt? What eyes? Whose breast?
Crumpled orphan, nembutal bed,
white hearse, Los Angeles,
DiMaggio! Los Angeles! Miller! Los Angeles! America!
That Death should seem the only protector –
That all arms should have faded, and the great cameras and lights
     become an inquisition and a torment –
That the many acquaintances, the autograph-hunters, the inflexible
     directors, the drive-in admirers should become a blur of
     incomprehension and pain –
That lonely Uncertainty should limp up, grinning, with bewildering
     barbiturates, and watch her undress and lie down and in her
     anguish
call for him! call for him to strengthen her with what could only
     dissolve her! A method
of dying, we are shaken, we see it. Strasberg!
Los Angeles! Olivier! Los Angeles! Others die
and yet by this death we are a little shaken, we feel it,
America.
Let no one say communication is a cantword.
They had to lift her hand from the bedside telephone.
But what she had not been able to say
perhaps she had said. 'All I had was my life.
I have no regrets, because if I made
any mistakes, I was responsible.
There is now – and there is the future.
What has happened is behind. So
it follows you around? So what?' – This
to a friend, ten days before.
And so she was responsible.
And if she was not responsible, not wholly responsible, Los Angeles?
     Los Angeles? Will it follow you around? Will the slow white
     hearse of the child of America follow you around?

from **Glasgow Sonnets**

5

'Let them eat cake' made no bones about it.
But we say let them eat the hope deferred
and that will sicken them. We have preferred
silent slipways to the riveters' wit.
And don't deny it – that's the ugly bit.
Ministers' tears might well have launched a herd
of bucking tankers if they'd been transferred
from Whitehall to the Clyde. And smiles don't fit
either. 'There'll be no bevvying' said Reid
at the work-in. But all the dignity you muster
can only give you back a mouth to feed
and rent to pay if what you lose in bluster
is no more than win patience with 'I need'
while distant blackboards use you as their duster.

6

The North Sea oil-strike tilts east Scotland up,
and the great sick Clyde shivers in its bed.
But elegists can't hang themselves on fled-
from trees or poison a recycled cup –
If only a less faint, shaky sunup
glimmered through the skeletal shop and shed
and men washed round the piers like gold and spread
golder in soul than Mitsubishi or Krupp –
The images are ageless but the thing
is now. Without my images the men
ration their cigarettes, their children cling
to broken toys, their women wonder when
the doors will bang on laughter and a wing
over the firth be simply joy again.

Glasgow 5 March 1971

With a ragged diamond
of shattered plate-glass
a young man and his girl
are falling backwards into a shop-window.
The young man's face
is bristling with fragments of glass
and the girl's leg has caught
on the broken window
and spurts arterial blood
over her wet-look white coat.
Their arms are starfished out
braced for impact,
their faces show surprise, shock,
and the beginning of pain.
The two youths who have pushed them
are about to complete the operation
reaching into the window
to loot what they can smartly.
Their faces show no expression.
It is a sharp clear night
in Sauchiehall Street.
In the background two drivers
keep their eyes on the road.

For Bonfires

I

The leaves are gathered, the trees are dying
for a time.
A seagull cries through white smoke in the garden fires
that fill the heavy air.
All day heavy air
is burning, a moody dog
sniffs and circles the swish of the rake.
In streaks of ash, the gardener drifting
ghostly, beats his hands, a cloud
of breath to the red sun.

II

An island in the city, happy demolition men
behind windowed hoardings – look at them
trailing drills through rubble dust, kicking rubble,
smoking leaning on a pick, putting the stub
over an ear and the hot yellow helmet over that,
whistling up the collapsing chimney, kicking the
ricochet, rattling the trail with
snakes of wire, slamming slabs
down, plaster, cornice, brick, brick
on broken brick and plaster dust,
sprawling with steaming cans and pieces
at noon, afternoon bare sweat shining
paths down chalky backs, coughing
in filtered sunshine, slithering, swearing,
joking, slowly stacking and building
their rubbish into a total bonfire.
Look at that Irishman, bending
in a beautiful arc to throw
the last black rafter to the top,
stands back, walks round it singing
as it crackles into flame – old doors,
old beams, boxes, window-frames,
a rag doll, sacks, flex, old newspapers,
burst shelves, a shoe, old dusters, rags of
wallpaper roses. And they all stand round,
and cheer the tenement to smoke.

III

In a galvanized bucket
the letters burn. They roar and twist
and the leaves curl back one by one.
They put out claws and scrape the iron
like a living thing,
but the scrabbling to be free soon subsides.
The black pages fuse
to a single whispering mass
threaded by dying tracks of gold.
Let them grow cold,
and when they're dead
quickly draw breath.

from **London**

3 The Post Office Tower
There is no other life,
and this is it.
Gold bars, thunder, gravity, wine, concrete, smoke.
And the blue pigeon London sky
hangs high heat on towers, a summer shower
on trees, its clouds
to swing over cranes
that swing slowly
blue vaguely.
We are drawn to the welder's star.
Ships we
half see.
Glass walls flash new cliffsides, brick-beds
brood with dust, red, grey, grey, blue.
Huge shadows skim the classic terraces.
Hunt sun hunt cloud, one long morning.

And life comes out on the roofs. A breeze
shakes raindrops from bonsai pines,
penthouse terrazzo gleams, dries, washed by heaven
around a fishpool: in dark glasses, a severe white suit
she stands by the marble verge and calls a dog, silently
twenty storeys above the roar.
On a roof southward, broken concrete
between two chimneys blossoms
in a line of washing, an old man
on a hard chair, his hands in his lap,
stares at nothing – linen flowers
tugging to be free. And like some fine insect
poised on a blackened outcrop of stone
a young man mends an aerial far down the central haze,
straddles a fire-escape in ice-blue jeans
and striped shirt, arms bare to the shoulder and his hair
is blown across his arms
as he moves the metal arms
into the path of their messages.
– And all that grace to dwindle to
a faded dressing-gown, a kitchen chair in the sun.
Years in shadows come low
over a penthouse garden dark with weeds,
phones ringing through empty rooms
for ashes thrown on the sea.

But still of life
not in clean waves and airs
the messages most heard
come to the tower
from asphalt and smoke
and break in rings
of strange accident
and mortal change
on the rain wet
silver bars.
It is its own
telegrams,
what mounts, what sighs,
what says it is
unaccountable
as feelings moved
by hair blown over
an arm in the wind.
In its acts
it rests there.

Spacepoem 3: Off Course

the golden flood   the weightless seat
the cabin song   the pitch black
the growing beard   the floating crumb
the shining rendezvous   the orbit wisecrack
the hot spacesuit   the smuggled mouth-organ
the imaginary somersault   the visionary sunrise
the turning continents   the space debris
the golden lifeline   the space walk
the crawling deltas   the camera moon
the pitch velvet   the rough sleep
the crackling headphone   the space silence
the turning earth   the lifeline continents
the cabin sunrise   the hot flood
the shining spacesuit   the growing moon
    the crackling somersault   the smuggled orbit
    the rough moon   the visionary rendezvous
    the weightless headphone   the cabin debris
    the floating lifeline   the pitch sleep
    the crawling camera   the turning silence
    the space crumb   the crackling beard
    the orbit mouth-organ   the floating song

The First Men on Mercury

– We come in peace from the third planet.
Would you take us to your leader?

– Bawr stretter! Bawr. Bawr. Stretterhawl?

– This is a little plastic model
of the solar system, with working parts.
You are here and we are there and we
are now here with you, is this clear?

– Gawl horrop. Bawr. Abawrhannahanna!

– Where we come from is blue and white
with brown, you see we call the brown
here 'land', the blue is 'sea', and the white
is 'clouds' over land and sea, we live
on the surface of the brown land,
all round is sea and clouds. We are 'men'.
Men come –

– Glawp men! Gawrbenner menko. Menhawl?

– Men come in peace from the third planet
which we call 'earth'. We are earthmen.
Take us earthmen to your leader.

– Thmen? Thmen? Bawr. Bawrhossop.
Yuleeda tan hanna. Harrabost yuleeda.

– I am the yuleeda. You see my hands,
we carry no benner, we come in peace.
The spaceways are all stretterhawn.

– Glawn peacemen all horrabhanna tantko!
Tan come at'mstrossop. Glawp yuleeda!

– Atoms are peacegawl in our harraban.
Menbat worrabost from tan hannahanna.

– You men we know bawrhossoptant. Bawr.
We know yuleeda. Go strawg backspetter quick.

– We cantantabawr, tantingko backspetter now!

– Banghapper now! Yes, third planet back.
Yuleeda will go back blue, white, brown
nowhanna! There is no more talk.

– Gawl han fasthapper?

– No. You must go back to your planet.
Go back in peace, take what you have gained
but quickly.

– Stretterworra gawl, gawl . . .

– Of course, but nothing is ever the same,
now is it? You'll remember Mercury.

The Moon February 1973

At the edge of the Sea of Serenity,
where the grey dust rises into foothills
of the Taurus Mountains, a confrontation
takes place. An unmanned, eight-wheeled steam pram,
Lunokhod-2, sophisticatedly clumsy as an
Emmett velocipede, has stopped its trundle
faced by a large, hard, blank, slab-like stone.
Busily it winks, and scans the monolith,
registering back to Tass
an impossible smoothness.
What crater could eject this unpitted stele
that stands marking nothing?
Too much simplicity is a headache for lunokhods,
and the moonrover has focused, in its frenzy for data,
on a spider-web of shadows and scratches at the base of the slab
which imagination might just read in Ventris mood
as K space BRI query space K query.

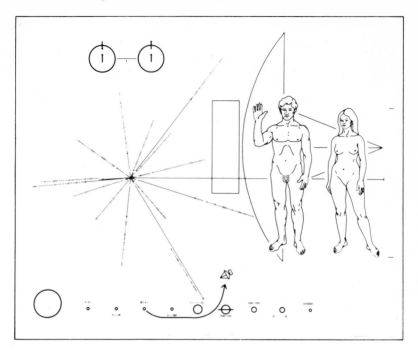

Translunar Space March 1972

The interior of Pioneer-10
as it courses smoothly beyond the Moon
at 31,000 miles an hour,
is calm and full of instruments.
No crew for the two-year trip to Jupiter,
but in the middle of the picture
a gold plaque, six inches by nine,
remedies the omission. Against a diagram
of the planets and pulsars of our solar system and galaxy,
and superimposed on an outline of the spacecraft
in which they are not travelling
(and would not be as they are shown
even if they were) two quaint nude figures
face the camera. A deodorized American man
with apologetic genitals and no pubic hair
holds up a banana-like right hand
in Indian greeting, at his side a woman,
smaller, and also with no pubic hair,
is not allowed to hold up her hand,
stands with one leg off-centre, and
is obviously an inferior sort
of the same species. However,
the male chauvinist pig
has a sullen expression, and the woman
is faintly smiling, so
interplanetary intelligences may still have homework.
Meanwhile, on to the Red Spot,
Pluto, and eternity.

Message Clear

```
    am              i
                              if
i am                      he
      he r        o
      h     ur    t
      the re           and
      he     re       and
      he re
  a               n   d
      th  e   r               e
i am      r                   ife
                  i n
            s       ion and
i                     d     i e
    am   e res   ect
    am   e res   ection
                    o           f
      the                     life
                  o           f
    m   e           n
          sur e
      the                 d    i e
i           s
            s   e t     and
i am the   sur         d
    a   t   res    t
                    o         life
i am  he r                    e
i a           ct
i       r  u     n
i  m   e   e      t
i             t              i e
i       s    t    and
i am th        o      th
i am    r         a
i am the  su    n
i am the  s       on
i am the  e   rect on      e if
i am    re      n     t
i am      s       a      fe
i am      s   e   n    t
i     he e           d
i    t e   s     t
```

```
i           re              a d
   a   th  re              a d
   a       s     t on                e
   a   t   re              a d
   a   th  r        on               e
i           resurrect
                          a       life
i am                   i  n       life
i am       resurrection
i am the resurrection and
i am
i am the resurrection and the life
```

Newmarket

```
tk–tke
tk–tke
tk–tke
tk–tke
tk–tke
tk–tke
tk–tke
hs–hss
hs–hss
tk–tke
tk–tke
ws–wss

shs–hs
ws–wss
tk–tke
tk–tke
kp–kpa
kp–kpa
kp–kpa
km–kmm
km–kmm
km–kmm
k–monn
k–monn
k–monn
k–monn
k–monn
a–tsit
```

Bradford June 1972

Dusty, bruised and grazed, and cut about a bit, but
cheerful, twenty men in white
are demolishing an old stone house
by karate.
They attack the worst part:
the thick cemented fireplace wall.
What a concert of chops is conducted
by him in the helmet, with KARATE INSTRUCTOR
across his back and Union Jacks and ideograms
along his sleeve: a deep-breathed plot
of timed and buttressed energies jabbing
one bare hand and two bare hands and
one bare foot and two bare feet and
one bare head at
stone: the pivot man,
swarming with badges, swings
on two friends' shoulders, clutches
their necks, leans back with knees
above his head and like a spring
uncoils two smart sharp whacks
from heels of steel,
and the wall keels.

Aviemore Invernessshire August 1971

The elephants are swaying from the ring
having left their mark. The audience
clap like mad and laugh and stamp.
A drunken ring-boy shakes his shovel
at the sway of faces as he stumbles
through steaming droppings, muttering.
His left hand brandishes derisively
a pair of stolen bright blue trousers.
The ringmaster strides to drag him off
as he V-signs the universe
and skids on spotlight dung. Elephants –
what's elephants to men yet?

Germany December 1970

A dead man is driving an old Mercedes
straight at a brick wall.
He is only one hour dead,
his hands have been laid
realistically on the wheel
by Herr Rudi Ulenhaut
the development engineer.
Under his dropped jaw
an inflatable safety air bag,
waiting to be tested on impact,
has just flown up
and broken his neck.

Chicago May 1971

The elegant vice-presidential office of US Steel
is the scene of a small ceremony.
A man has placed a miniature coffin
on the vice-president's couch, and in the coffin
you can see frog, perch, crawfish, dead.
They have swallowed the laborious effluent
of US Steel in Lake Michigan.
The man is poised ready to run,
wrinkling his nose as he pours from a held-out bottle
a dark brown viscous Michigan sludge
over the vice-president's white rug. This is
the eco-man. On the table his card,
The Fox.

from Interferences: a sequence of nine poems

1
not to be deflected
the arrow, puffed up
speeding busily
straight to its
                targjx

4
'it was a Roman soldier'
he cried, his fist

'it was our neighbour'
pounded the table

'it was a visitor'
dropped wearily

and she took his hand
placed it on her womb

'I am your virgian bride'
with a smile worlds away

5
brigantine tacking
canvas set
in calm seas
off the Azores
December 1872
a sorry zigzag
we boarded her
in the queen's name
found no one
ghost ship
all shipshape
log written up
no mutiny
no tempest
no sickness
no ghosts
captain's wife
had a sewing-machine
with a phial of oil
upright and ready
she had left her task
in no disorder
all was dry
all was clean
the sails whole
the hull smooth
rocking to
and fro quietly
fourteen persons
in earth or sea
or air or space
or in that place
where their ship is
the Mar Celste

9
bringing you live
the final preparations
for this great mission
should be coasting
the rings of Saturn
two years time
cloudless sky, and
an unparalleled
world coverage
we have countdown
    ten
may not have told you
    nine
the captain's mascot
    eight
miniaturized gonk
    seven
chief navigator
    six
had twins Tuesday
    five
the Eiffel Tower for
    four
comparison, gantries
    three
aside, so the fuel
    two
huge cloud of
    one
perfect
    a half
I don't quite
    a quarter
something has clearly
    an eighth
we do not have lift-off
    a sixteenth
we do not have lift-off
    a thirty-second
we do not have lift-off
    a sixty-fourth
we do not have lift-off
    a hundred and twenty-eighth
wo de nat hove loft-iff

NOTES

Charles Causley

Reservoir Street
2   *the Strike* the General Strike.
     bubbling a hint here of the behaviour of tar in very hot weather. Cf. Keith Waterhouse, *There is a Happy Land*, ch. 1, Longman.
28   *cloam* clay, which in Cornwall is white.

Death of a Poet
The poet was Louis MacNeice, who died in 1963.

The Question
This seems to me an outstanding example of Charles Causley's mastery of the anonymous and riddling idioms of religious folk tradition. Cf. 'Down in yon forest there stands a hall', *Oxford Book of Carols*, no. 61, Oxford University Press.

In Coventry
1   *ruddled* stained red – blood was spilt in the Blitz. I suspect also a hint of the destructiveness of 'urban renewal'.
3   *cracked* also means 'potty' or 'daft'. This reading is reinforced by lines 5, 6, 8 and 17.
5–6   *Christ hung down* . . . a reference to Graham Sutherland's tapestry which hangs at the east end of the cathedral.
7–8   *his crown of thorns* literally true: the large thorn-crown which 'decorates' the entrance of the chapel was made in the workshops of the Royal Engineers.
10   *retablos* decorative panels.
19   *chunnered* chundered, remonstrated.

Immunity
4   *tickler* cigarette made from duty-free tobacco.
5   *sick-bay tiffy* sick-berth attendant.
6   *quack* ship's medical officer.
14   *pusser* purser.
15   *Hippocrates* reputed founder of medical science.
20   *pulled up the hook* weighed anchor.
25   *Kos* island off Greece.

At the Grave of John Clare and Helpston
'Helpston' is the poem I wrote about returning to the place twenty years or so after writing 'At the Grave of John Clare'. . . . Clare is a key man with me.
John Clare was born in Helpston, Northamptonshire, in 1793 and was buried there in 1864 after twenty-three years in Northampton Lunatic Asylum. See John Clare, *Selected Poems and Prose*, ed. Eric Robinson and Geoffrey Summerfield, Oxford University Press.

Ou Phrontis
The words 'Ou Phrontis' were carved by T. E. Lawrence over the door of
his cottage at Clouds Hill, Dorset. They come from the story in Herodotus,
on which this poem is based.

Song of the Dying Gunner A.A. 1
A.A. anti-aircraft.
13 *Aggie Weston* 'Aggie Weston's' is the familiar term used by sailors to
describe the hostels founded in many seaports by Dame Agnes Weston.
Guz naval wireless call sign: G-U-Z. 'Guz' is naval slang for Devonport.

Death of an Aircraft
The Cretan Campaign was a savagely fought campaign in which the
Germans used paratroopers in great numbers.

Mary, Mary Magdalene
Charles Causley composed the following tune for this poem–song:

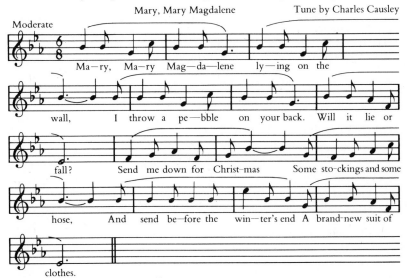

Mary, Mary Magdalene   Tune by Charles Causley

Ma—ry, Ma—ry Mag—da—lene ly—ing on the wall, I throw a pe—bble on your back. Will it lie or fall? Send me down for Christ-mas Some sto-ckings and some hose, And send be—fore the win—ter's end A brand-new suit of clothes.

Chief Petty Officer
15 *Crippen-collar* the high wing-collar made notorious, in folk-memory, by the
widely circulated photograph of Charles Crippen, the wife-murderer.
26 *Lay* a neatly deliberate error for 'lie'.
39 *tot-time* time for the daily issue of a tot of free rum.
40 *Jutland* the scene of major naval battles in World War One. The 'ruffling' is,
therefore, the effect of memories.

The Reverend Sabine Baring-Gould
The Reverend Sabine Baring-Gould (1834–1924) was Rector for forty-
three years at Lewtrenchard in Devon. He is the author of the hymn
'Onward Christian Soldiers'.

Thom Gunn

Tamer and Hawk

9   *seeled* to seel is to close the eye of the hawk by stitching its eyelids together as part of the process of training it.

The Discovery of the Pacific

The distinctiveness of a poet is often most keenly sensed by playing a poem off against another poet's work. One knows more surely what kind of poet Thom Gunn is, and what kind of poet Seamus Heaney is, by comparing this poem to Seamus Heaney's 'Westering', p. 118.

10   *resin-smell and to the firs' slight sound* an indication that, after the dry parched flat-lands, they have reached the forests of California.

20   *iceplant* a prolific succulent plant that grows rapidly in sandy soil. Many motorways in California have been softened by its use; visually, it resembles a larger form of mesembryanthemum, with spectacular brittle flowers, and thick fleshy leaves.

23–4   Here, the metaphor of pause, rest, union and consummation is the perfect climax of the metaphor of movement that carries the whole poem. (This fine control of sustaining metaphor, achieving almost mythic dimensions, is seen, in a different way, in Seamus Heaney's 'Rite of Spring', p. 111.) As even this small selection shows, the metaphor of motion is a recurrent feature of Thom Gunn's sense of experience.

Listening to Jefferson Airplane

In the 1960s, the great years of Filmore West, the Bay Area in general, and San Francisco in particular, was a mecca for pop musicians.

Apartment Cats

7   *re-enact Ben Hur* the cats perform a mock-heroic version of the celebrated chariot-race in the spectacular epic film.

The Produce District

California is the world's largest market-garden, and the Produce District of San Francisco is their equivalent of our Covent Garden.

2   *wrecking* demolition.

8   *trucks* lorries.

Epitaph for Anton Schmidt

Gunn, no less than Causley, Hughes or Mitchell, has attended to war: in his case, his attention has been characteristically turned on questions of will, motive, intention and choice.

10   *determine* there are several resonant meanings lying in this word in this context.

Innocence

Compare Norman MacCaig's remarks (p. 162).

My Sad Captains

The title is from *Antony and Cleopatra*. In Act III, Scene 13, Antony says to Cleopatra:

I will be treble-sinewed, hearted, breathed,
And fight maliciously; for when mine hours
Were nice and lucky, men did ransom lives

Of me for jests. But now I'll set my teeth,
And send to darkness all that stop me. Come,
Let's have one other gaudy night. Call to me
All my sad captains, fill our bowls once more.
Let's mock the midnight bell.

And what does 'sad' mean? Consider the following definitions from the
Shorter Oxford English Dictionary:

1. Settled, firmly established, in purpose or condition.
2. Steadfast, firm, constant.
3. Of trustworthy character and judgement; grave, serious.

In Gunn's case those whom he invokes, or 'calls', in order to 'mock the
midnight bell', to withstand darkness and melancholy, are from two
worlds: friends from the world of his own, actual, life; and, from the world
of the past, those who, though literally dead, are still alive to him, and not
merely names on the spines of books.
Compare Wordsworth, *The Prelude*, Book III, lines 608 ff.:

> 'And oftentimes do flit
> Remembrances before me of old men –
> Old humorists, who have been long in their graves,
> And having almost in my mind put off
> Their human names, have into phantoms passed
> Of texture midway between life and books'

17 *disinterested* unbiased by thought of personal gain.

Claus Von Stauffenberg
16 A reminder of the conspiracy against the tyranny of Caesar.

Flying Above California
2 *tawny* in the summer, the grass of the hills of California is burnt to a light
brown, tawny, colour.
4 *loquat* a form of Japonica.
7 *Mediterranean* many of the place names of California are Spanish, dating
from the Spanish colonization.

Considering the Snail
18 *that deliberate progress* compare the last line of 'Epitaph for Anton Schmidt'.

'Blackie, the Electric Rembrandt'
The scene, for those who have not witnessed it, is a tattoo-parlour. Instead
of a brush, the artist wields an electric 'pen' which punctures the skin. The
pigment is then introduced into the wound.

Rites of Passage
The term is from anthropology and is used of those moments of transition
from one stage of life to another. Many 'primitive' cultures have complex
rituals for entering adulthood. We have the 'key of the door', the vote and
the 'age of consent'.

ROBERT DUNCAN **Second Take on** *Rites of Passage*
This poem is included at Thom Gunn's request. Starting from Gunn's poem,
Robert Duncan has re-presented the situation from the father's point of
view.

JOHN DOWLAND (?) **Song**
This Elizabethan song, made famous by Alfred Deller, the counter-tenor, is
included at Thom Gunn's request.

Street Song
I consciously wrote my poem with such a poem as Dowland's in mind. . . .
It is a poem not taking sides. It is no more an encouragement to take
drugs than 'Porphyria's Lover' is an encouragement to murder.
6 *Keys lids acid and speed* Slang words for various drugs. 'Keys' and 'lids'
   refer to marijuana, 'acid' to LSD and 'speed' to amphetamines.

Seamus Heaney

Follower
'Follower' was meant to turn into a love poem but ended up telling more
about me than any biographical note.

Gone
11 *must* mustiness, a smell of mould.

The Salmon Fisher to the Salmon
9 A reference to Walton's *The Compleat Angler*.

Undine
The title refers to one of the pagan water-spirits.

The Last Mummer
Mummer's plays – boisterous, knock-about and savage folk-plays, usually
performed at Christmas or Easter, are thought to be survivals of primordial
seasonal rituals, performed to ensure the return of the sun, after a long
dark winter, and the success of the harvest. They therefore centre on
resurrection and fertility, and most versions contain a death followed by a
miraculous re-birth. R. J. Tiddy collected many versions in Oxfordshire and
Gloucestershire before the First World War, but his work was cut short
when he was killed on active service. They have survived in various places
in an attenuated form, and some have been recently revived. (See *Voices*,
Book II, Penguin, pp. 167 ff. and the notes.) Although Heaney's poetry is
rooted in Ireland, he seems here to be repaying a debt to a peculiarly
English poet – Edward Thomas. The primordial subject, and the naturally
pious *frisson*, the sense of magical power, with which Heaney presents it –
these are very close to the best of Edward Thomas. In the third section of
the poem is a reference to the mummer's crucial function – to point
forward from the depths of winter to the future spring and rebirth. Compare
the custom of first-footing. What I find peculiarly exciting here is Heaney's
realization of the potency of the pagan, pre-Christian (pre-television!)
culture.
39 *monstrance* a transparent or open vessel of gold or silver to hold the
    sacramental host.

Toome
2–3 The meaning of the second line will be clear if you speak the third line,
     slowly and quietly.

11 *torc* prehistoric bracelet or necklace, made out of twisted metal, often gold. The Celts produced fine examples.

The Tollund Man

Tollund man was discovered in a Danish peat bog by two farmers on 8 May 1950. He was so remarkably well preserved that the farmers imagined he must be the victim of a recent murder. In fact, he was 2000 years old, an inhabitant of the Iron Age, maintained in almost perfect condition by the peat. Investigation revealed more details. Although it at first appeared that the Tollund man was in a sleeping position, it was later discovered that he had a rope around his neck and that he had died by hanging. The contents of his stomach were also analysed: between twelve and twenty-four hours before his death he had eaten a meal consisting of a gruel made from barley, linseed, 'gold-of-pleasure', knotweed and other sorts of weed common on ploughed land. The recipe was used to produce an exact copy of Tollund man's meal and was served up on television to two famous archaeologists, Sir Mortimer Wheeler and Dr Glyn Daniel. It was not appreciated, and the eminent gentlemen were obliged to get rid of the taste by taking a large swill of good Danish brandy from a cow horn. Sir Mortimer declared that it would have been punishment enough for Tollund man to have had to eat this gruel for the rest of his life, however terrible his crime. For more details of the fascinating discoveries in Danish peat bogs see P. V. Glob, *The Bog People*, Faber; Paladin.

Augury

10 A perfect example of Heaney's deft use of metaphor: they stood, literally, on a catwalk; but the poem 'expands' to contain us all: we all hang on a 'trembling catwalk', an earth poised between hope of restoration and final ruination.

Dedicatory Poem from **Wintering Out**

7 *déjà-vu* something that you have a sense of having seen before, even if that is actually impossible.

Ted Hughes

The Rock

4 *memento mundi* a reminder of the world.

The Thought-Fox

An animal I never succeeded in keeping alive is the fox. I was always frustrated: twice by a farmer, who killed cubs I had caught before I could get to them, and once by a poultry keeper who freed my cub while his dog waited. Years after those events I was sitting up late one snowy night in dreary lodgings in London. I had written nothing for a year or so but that night I got the idea I might write something and I wrote in a few minutes the following poem: the first 'animal' poem I ever wrote. Here it is – 'The Thought-Fox' . . .

This poem does not have anything you could easily call a meaning. It is about a fox, obviously enough, but a fox that is both a fox and not a fox. What sort of a fox is it that can step right into my head where presumably

it still sits . . . smiling to itself when the dogs bark. It is both a fox and a
spirit. It is a real fox; as I read the poem I see it move, I see it setting its
prints, I see its shadow going over the irregular surface of the snow. The
words show me all this, bringing it nearer and nearer. It is very real to me.
The words have made a body for it and given it somewhere to walk.

If, at the time of writing this poem, I had found livelier words, words that
could give me much more vividly its movements, the twitch and craning of
its ears, the slight tremor of its hanging tongue and its breath making little
clouds, its teeth bared in the cold, the snow-crumbs dropping from its pads
as it lifts each one in turn, if I could have got the words for all this, the fox
would probably be even more real and alive to me now, than it is as I read
the poem. Still, it is there as it is. If I had not caught the real fox there in
the words I would never have saved the poem. I would have thrown it into
the wastepaper basket as I have thrown so many other hunts that did not
get what I was after. As it is, every time I read the poem the fox comes up
again out of the darkness and steps into my head. And I suppose that long
after I am gone, as long as a copy of the poem exists, every time anyone
reads it the fox will get up somewhere out in the darkness and come
walking towards them.

Song
Ted Hughes's earliest currently published poem, written when he was
eighteen.

The Jaguar
Ted Hughes wrote this when he worked as a dishwasher in the London Zoo.
He could see the caged jaguar from his kitchen sink. See 'Second Glance
at a Jaguar', page 151.

Griefs for Dead Soldiers
The tragedy and the tragic legacies of the First World War – the 'Great
War' as it used to be called – have been very present to Ted Hughes's
generation. They came to Adrian Mitchell through the poetry of Wilfred
Owen; to Ted Hughes through the conversation of his father; to others of
us, through the silences of our fathers. See 'Out', page 153; Charles
Causley's observations, page 20; and Norman MacCaig's 'Among the
Talk and the Laughter', page 181.

Six Young Men
The six men were friends of Ted Hughes's father, and the actual photograph
had been taken just before the war.

Crow Hill
'Crow Hill' is near the home of the Brontes, on the Yorkshire Moors. Ted
Hughes has remarked that Crow Hill lies at the meeting point of winds
from all directions; it rains on about 265 days of the year. Why, Ted Hughes
asked on one occasion, **do people go on living there?**

Esther's Tomcat
Esther, the wife of an engraver who was producing a series of animal
drawings, was finding suitable pieces of prose and poetry to match the
engravings. She could find nothing on tomcats, so Ted Hughes wrote this for
her.

Relic
Cf. T. S. Eliot's *Four Quartets*: 'The Dry Salvages'; and John Keats's
'Epistle to Reynolds' (March 1818):

> I saw
> Too far into the sea; where every maw
> The greater on the lesser feeds evermore:
> But I saw too distinct into the core
> Of an eternal fierce destruction . . .

Witches
When Ted Hughes once read this poem in public, he observed that it
depended on the hypothesis that telepathy 'works', that malice can be
projected intensely and concentratedly onto and into another person, and
harm or damage them.

13   *As if they had dreamed all* cf. Vernon Watkins:

> My quarrel with these Londoners
> Is that they try
> To substitute psychology
> For the naked sky
> Of metaphysical movement,
> And drain the blood dry.
> All is materialism, all
> The catchwords they strew
> Alien to the blood of man.

From 'Yeats in Dublin', *The Lamp and the Veil*, Faber, 1945.

Pike
Ted Hughes once wrote as follows about this poem: I used to be a very
keen angler for pike, as I still am when I get the chance, and I did most of
my early fishing in a quiet small lake, really a large pond. This pond went
down to a great depth in one place. Sometimes, on hot days, we would see
something like a railway sleeper lying near the surface, and there certainly
were huge pike in that pond. I suppose they are even bigger by now.
Recently I felt like doing some pike fishing, but in circumstances where
there was no chance of it, and over the days, as I remember the extreme
pleasures of that sport, bits of the following poem began to arrive. As you
will see, by looking at the place in my memory very hard and very
carefully and by using the words that grew naturally out of the pictures and
feelings, I captured not just a pike, I captured the whole pond, including
the monsters I never even hooked.

In a recent letter, Ted Hughes describes the pond as now a rubbish dump,
pretty well, with an oily puddle in the bottom.

Second Glance at a Jaguar
'Second Glance at a Jaguar' is a curiosity for me. I wrote it while standing
in front of the jaguar's cage, in Regent's Park Zoo, in direct contradiction
to my notions of how poetry ought to be composed. It includes one line
rejected from 'The Jaguar' eight years earlier.

Wilfred Owen's Photographs
The title works by analogy: Owen carried round with him photographs of
men wounded on the Western front in the First World War and while he
was on leave, back in England, he insisted on showing the people at home
photographs of the realities of the war which had been presented as
glorious and patriotic by the government's propaganda.

Out
Ted Hughes in March 1963 described this poem as **an attempt to have done
with the First World War.**

Pibroch
In the Gaelic bagpipe tradition, the pibroch – an extended composition
based on an air and variations, made according to an elaborate set of rules
– is part of the *ceol mor* (big music) as distinct from *ceol beag* (little music).
Traditionally, the great pipers confined their repertoire to the 'big music':
the little music comprised dance tunes, and other light-weight elements. In
general, the effect of the pibroch is that of a dirge or a lament. If you wish
to hear a fine pibroch played supremely well, listen to John Burgess playing
'The desperate battle of the birds', on Topic 12T199.

Gnat-Psalm
This is a poem that Ted Hughes has re-worked, and the present text differs
from that given in *Wodwo*, pp. 179–81. The first three stanzas exemplify the
distinctively virtuoso impressionism that the subject seems to have inspired
in several poets. Compare Denise Levertov's *Six Variations*.
49 *Hasids* 'chasid' is a Hebrew word meaning 'pious' or 'pious one'. The
Hasidic movement in the Jewish religion began in the eighteenth century,
teaching simple faith and joyous worship rather than formal learning. The
Hasids were the leaders of this movement and were looked upon as
particularly holy men by their followers.

Norman MacCaig

Byre
11 *Aphrodite* the goddess of love.
12 *slaver* after 'swinging' and 'silver' many eyes anticipate or begin to expect
'salver'. Hence a pleasurable surprise in 'slaver', and the transformation of
the word – usually unpleasant in tone – into something fine and beautiful.
Compare D. H. Lawrence:

When a boy of eight sees a horse, he doesn't see the correct biological object we
intend him to see. He sees a big living presence of no particular shape with hair
dangling from its neck and four legs. If he puts two eyes in the profile, he is quite
right. Because he does *not* see with optical, photographic vision . . . The child is *not* a
little camera.
(*Fantasia of the Unconscious*)

Visiting Hour
38 *and fruitless fruits* note how the growing tension of the poem comes to a
head in the collision of 'fruitless' and 'fruits'.

Brooklyn Cop

3 *hieroglyphs* because his eyes are inscrutable, impossible to read.

14 *nightstick* truncheon

Basking Shark

2 *slounge* unexpected, slightly disconcerting, is well placed to express the disconcertment and also to compel a special sharpness of attention. The 'meaning' is best found, not in a dictionary, but in rowing. See the similar effect of 'shoggled' (line 7).

Wild Oats

3 *gyroscopes* put a spinning gyroscope on a piece of string or on the end of a pencil and watch the mixture of equilibrium and instability. The slight menace of its motion is a nice analogue for the postures of male pigeons.

Odd Man Out

Notice how the 'persona' of the poem is enforced by the sheer contrariness of line 15 and the neat ambiguity of 'get along' (line 18). Survive or disappear?

Moon-Landing

3 *the apple exploded* obviously a reference to the famous apple which (or so it is said) suggested the law of gravity to Newton by falling on his head. But Newton's work extended that of Galileo and Copernicus, and extended our sense of the universe and of our place in it.

New Tables

On reading this poem I asked Norman MacCaig about his familiarity with the work of the Czech poet, Miroslav Holub. He replied, **Have you a litmus paper in your skull? Or a radar of some sort or another?** No, but see such poems as 'Žito the Magician', 'Inventions' and 'Model of Man' in Holub's *Selected Poems*, Penguin.

Television Studio

7 *Cousteau* Cousteau is both a 'star' of television and also an aquanaut who has used cameras with new kinds of ingenuity. He is therefore an appropriate part of the poem's sustained fantasy.

Aunt Julia

The tensions in the minds of Scots writers between the claims of Gaelic (their native language) and English (the colonizer's language) are explored in depth in Iain Crichton Smith's poems 'Shall Gaelic Die?' (*Selected Poems*, Gollancz). Crichton Smith writes:

Words rise out of the country. They are around us. . . . He who loses his language loses his world. The Highlander who loses his language loses his world. 'Shall Gaelic die?' A hundred years from now who will say these words? Who will say, 'Co their?' Who? The voice of the owl.

'Co their?' is Gaelic for 'Who will say?'

Changes in the Same Thing

11–14 We need not assume here that MacCaig is speaking from a literal acceptance of Genesis, but rather the Biblical myth is still of service to the poetic imagination.

Early Sunday Morning, Edinburgh

5   *stratch* I hope we can appreciate 'stratch' as a gift. Maybe we also can enjoy using it. I doubt if we shall need to consult a dictionary.

16   *Sacraments* appropriate not merely to the church-going Sunday morning, but also to what people's faces 'give' to MacCaig. See section 2 of the *Shorter Oxford English Dictionary* entry for 'Sacrament'.

Incident

14–15   *the marvellous world of possibility* the marvels of the fantasy (lines 7–9) are marvellous in a different way from the marvels of the possible: the possible marvels are no less marvellous than the impossible marvels. When people talk abstractly about poets 'keeping the language alive', think of MacCaig's renovation of the word 'marvellous' in line 14.

July Day Spectacular

4   *flies* screens and curtains, as on a stage. Just as concealed lamps shine from behind the flies, so the sun shines from behind clouds.

8   *oystercatchers* very spectacular, noisy, excitable birds that frequent rivers and shorelines. Notice how MacCaig gives them a line to themselves – one of the advantages of free verse that MacCaig clearly enjoys exploiting. **As for why I turned (not altogether) from metrics to free verse, I have no idea. It just happened, without wish, never mind calculation or intention. Recently I've been writing a good deal in metrical forms, usually with rhymes but playing around a good deal with the strictness of both.**

Adrian Mitchell

Time and Motion Study

The imaginations which people have of one another are the *solid facts* of society. . . . I do not mean merely that society must be studied by the imagination – that is true of all investigations in their higher reaches – but that the *object* of study is primarily an imaginative idea or group of ideas in the mind, that we have to imagine imaginations. The intimate grasp of any social fact will be found to require that we divine what men think of one another.
(Charles Horton Cooley, *Human Nature and the Social Order*)

The Castaways or Vote for Caliban

Caliban is the monster in Shakespeare's *The Tempest*.

Veteran with a Head Wound

41   *Boswell* James Boswell (1740–1795) was the indefatigable biographer of Samuel Johnson, seeming at times to note down, or memorize, every word that Johnson uttered.

Open Day at Porton

Porton Down is the site of the British government's biological and chemical warfare research establishment. The joke of the title is, of course, that 'security' at Porton is as tight as anywhere in the world.

Final Chant

This is part of Adrian Mitchell's commentary for Roy Battersby's film *The Body* (Kestrel Films), one of the finest documentaries ever made.
Appreciation of the poem is only really possible by seeing/hearing it work in the film, but try to imagine it!

Briefing
The instructor teaching his charges how to stone someone is no more preposterous or absurd (or incredible) than many an army weapons instructor. Note how in the last stanza no one (except the instructor) is above suspicion.

Hear the Voice of the Critic
Adrian Mitchell catches the carping, negative, dismissive voice of the critic – he who lives for 'flat white plates'. On poetry critics in particular cf. his poem:

To Ian Hamilton and A. Alvarez, Poetry Reviewers
Get your blue hands
off the hot skin of poetry.

The Marie Lloyd Song
Marie Lloyd (1870–1922) was perhaps the best-known and best-loved of the old music hall comediennes. The *Concise Dictionary of National Biography* says that she was 'notable for cheery vitality, knowledge of vulgar, especially cockney, English, and swift, significant expression'.
10 *Sigmund Freud* (1856–1939) the founder of psychoanalysis.
17 *Dylan Thomas* (1914–1953) the Welsh poet.
18 *Nye Bevan* (1897–1960) the Welsh politician and architect of the National Health Service.

Bessie Smith in Yorkshire
Bessie Smith (1898–1937) was the greatest of the jazz blues singers.

Edwin Morgan

Trio
12 *Orphean sprig* of Orpheus, the Greek god of music.
18 *this march of three* whether or not Edwin Morgan intended an echo of the three magi I have no idea; but I certainly feel such a resonance, gently ironic.

The Suspect
This poem opens itself up interestingly if it is read aloud. There are several voices: the suspect's, the policeman's, the interior voice of the suspect, either addressing the dead man or talking to himself.

Glasgow Green
24–7 *the sweat/is real . . . is the real* cf. Edwin Morgan's observation on page 229 about 'the grit of the facts of the case' and 'the absolute force of what actually happens'. For an extended exploration of the act of attending to the real, see James Agee, *Let us Now Praise Famous Men*, Panther.

In the Snack-Bar
28–9 *I concentrate/my life to his* not merely attending to the task of helping him, but also imagining his life. Cf. Sartre: 'There are men who die without – save for brief and terrifying flashes of illumination – ever having suspected what the *Other* is. The horizons of my life are infinitely shrunk.'

The Death of Marilyn Monroe

2 *nembutal* Marilyn Monroe died of an overdose of sleeping drugs.

4 *DiMaggio* Joe DiMaggio, a celebrated baseball player, ex-husband.
Miller Arthur Miller, celebrated playwright, ex-husband.
Los Angeles home of Hollywood, the city in which she worked and died.

7 *the drive-in admirers* in California you can drive your car into the open-air space in front of a screen and watch movies under the stars. Just as you drive into a drive-in hamburger stall for a hamburger without having to leave your car, so you can watch Marilyn Monroe. The Hamburger, Marilyn Monroe – both are consumables.

9–10 *A method/of dying* method here is in oblique reference to the very naturalistic and improvisatory method of acting that Marilyn Monroe studied at Lee Strasberg's Actor's Studio in New York City.

Glasgow Sonnet 5

1 *'Let them eat cake'* the words are those of Marie Antoinette when told that the French peasants had no bread. At least she didn't conceal her meaning (her contempt, her ignorance) in bureaucratic jargon or euphemism.

9 *bevvying* drinking
Reid Jimmy Reid, the trade union leader, possibly the best political rhetorician since the death of Aneurin Bevan.

10 *work-in* the work-in occurred when the management closed the shipyard, but the workers stayed on and insisted on working under the management of a workers' committee.

Glasgow Sonnet 6

3 *elegists* those who express sorrowful regret or anguish, traditionally bards or poets.

8 *Mitsubishi or Krupp* hyper-rich Japanese and German industrialists. Krupp achieved notoriety for employing Jewish slave-labour in his factories during the Nazi regime. He was subsequently rehabilitated into respectability.

13 *a wing* also casts shadows as it passes over.

Glasgow 5 March 1971

This is one of Edwin Morgan's 'instamatic poems'. In these he pushes his actuality towards an almost split second photographic sharpness – the action arrested in a flash. He, as it were, 'makes up' nothing, simply turns a camera-eye on the event, caught in the act. Other instamatic poems, many of them derived from newspaper reports or photographs, are 'Translunar Space March 1972', 'The Moon February 1973', Aviemore Invernessshire August 1971', 'Germany December 1970' and 'Chicago May 1971'.

Spacepoem 3: Off Course

When I read this poem with American students, they recalled Apollo XIII, and so understood the dark meaning of that indentation at line 15.

21 *the floating song* in folk song, a floater is a stanza that becomes detached from its original song, floats around, and can end up heaven knows where.

The First Men on Mercury

Try reading this aloud with a friend. Resist the temptation to change sides, or the evolution of the poem's surprise will get out of control. In this poem Edwin Morgan's interest in translation and his delight in space exploration achieve a very happy unity.

The Moon February 1973

11 *stele* an upright slab of stone with inscriptions.

16 *Ventris* Michael Ventris, the brilliant linguist–cryptographer who cracked the mystery of one of the early Mediterranean languages which had baffled experts for many years.

17 If you're still puzzled, think of *2001*.

Translunar Space March 1972

[The] primary goal is to send back to earth, some two years hence, close-up pictures and scientific observations of Jupiter, largest planet of the solar system. But a more exciting – albeit uncertain – mission is to announce to some distant civilization that we are here. It is the first official effort on the part of mankind to draw attention to itself. As the vehicle, Pioneer 10, passes Jupiter, the gravity of that planet will seize it and hurl it out of the solar system. It will sail indefinitely through the vast reaches of the Milky Way Galaxy, carrying a message in the form of a gold-coated aluminum plate, for any members of other planetary civilizations who may happen to encounter it. Scientists agree, however, that the chances are very slim indeed.

The message is designed to be decipherable to any scientist, regardless of his physiognomy, history or location in space and time. The symbol, upper left, draws attention to the two states of the hydrogen atom as the unit of time (radio frequency) and distance (wavelength) to be used. The star-like diagram shows the position of the earth relative to fourteen pulsars. These are stars that emit radio pulses at regular (though in some cases slowly changing) rhythms. Solid lines indicate the relative distances of these pulsars. The dashed extensions of these lines are marked with tics indicating the rate at which that pulsar is pulsing. The rate could be used to identify each pulsar, much as each lighthouse has its characteristic rhythm. Since a few pulsars are slowing their rate, the message also indicates roughly the time of launch.

The long horizontal line extending to the right behind the two figures indicates the direction of the centre of the Milky Way Galaxy. The figures stand in front of a schematic diagram of the spacecraft with its dish-shaped antenna to give an idea of the dimensions and appearance of earth's inhabitants. The man's hand is raised in friendly salute. Below is a representation of the solar system with the sun at the left, showing that Pioneer 10 was launched from the third planet out from the sun and then was thrown out of the system by Jupiter's gravity.

(Walter Sullivan)

Message Clear

This poem was first published in *The Times Literary Supplement*, 13 January 1966. On 20 January the *TLS* published the following two letters:

May I congratulate Edwin Morgan on typing 'I am the resurrection and the life' – after fifty-four unsuccessful attempts?

As a one-time two-finger man myself, I feel that we should all join in giving him a big hand.

ARNOLD HYDE
27 Viceroy Court, Wilmslow Road,
Didsbury, Manchester 20.

The poem 'Message Clear' by Edwin Morgan, published in your issue of 13 January, is curiously moving. I asked myself (with due reservations about the usefulness of the question) if this is really a poem. As a whole it has no linguistic reverberation, merely a visual presence. It could not be perpetuated vocally, or in the memory. It seems to be a piece of graphic art with visual rhythms evolving into a caption – a diagram exploding into a familiar quotation from the Bible. Certainly it irritated me at first (all that trouble with the print to render an already familiar quotation) but the central statement is given a context. The corruption, or rather erosion, of words in the body of the poem gives it a new vitality, when it finally emerges. We feel how patiently, even passionately, the poet (arranger? cryptographer?) has felt his way towards this. So that in this case the result is not merely a puzzle, or a piece of letter *trompe-l'oeil*. But it may be only a lucky spurt, a wise selection for publication from a usually unrewarding genre that is normally more at home in the graphic magazines. The graphic art has probably more to gain from a marriage with poetry than poetry from intercourse with graphics.

My summing up on this piece is that it is 'I am the Resurrection and the Life' interestingly presented: a Good Book dust cover design. Perhaps a typographer would have done it even better.

JACK BEVAN
77 Penkell Road,
Wallasey, Cheshire.

On 3 February the *TLS* published the following letter:

Can it be that both your correspondents (*TLS*, 20 January) entirely missed the point of Mr Edwin Morgan's 'Message Clear'? Mr Hyde's note, while extremely witty, was quite irrelevant. Mr Bevan at least brought some painstaking thought to bear upon it; but it seems he was unable to penetrate beyond the 'visual presence' on the page. His allusion to 'graphics', 'typography', 'visual rhythms', and so on, make this plain.

I would suggest that this poem has nothing essential to do with its typography. (One looked at first for a connection with the seventeenth-century conceit, as in George Herbert with his 'Wings' and 'Altars' shaped visually upon the page; but there is nothing so obvious here.) The purpose of the 'design' surely is to suggest the fragmentation and fumbling search – infinite trial and error, perhaps – of all mankind before finally the Message *is* Clear.

It seems incredible that one should have to spell this out in so many words (complete with upper case and punctuation) – but how else to demonstrate to Mr Bevan and others the 'linguistic reverberations' and the poem's capacity of 'perpetuation' either 'vocally or in the memory'?

The Hopkins-like echoes in the first few lines lend compelling force at the outset – but Mr Morgan then proceeds on his way with plenty of force of his own:

Am I?
                              if
I am he,
Hero,
Hurt
There and
Here and here
And there,
I am rife
                              in
Sion and
I die:
Am ere sect,
Am ere section
          of
The life
          of
               men.
     Sure,
The die
Is set and

I am the surd –
At rest

                    O life!

I am here:
I act,
I run,
I meet,
I tie,
I stand;
I am Thoth,
I am Ra,
I am the Sun
I am the Son –
I am the erect one: if
I am rent,
I am safe
I am sent,
I heed,
I test.
I read
  A thread,
  A stone,
  A tread,
  A throne.
I resurrect

                    a life:

I am in life;
I am resurrection;
I am the resurrection and
I am;
I am the resurrection and the life.

Perhaps Mr Bevan would admit that this, too is moving; although much of what Mr Morgan was trying to do is lost in such a 'translation'.

HEATHER BREMER
2 Bretland Road,
Tunbridge Wells, Kent.

On 10 February the *TLS* published the following letter:

May I correct two of the phrases in Heather Bremer's 'translation' of my poem 'Message Clear'? In lines 13 and 14 of her version, 'Am ere sect' and 'Am ere section' should read 'A mere sect' and 'A mere section'.

EDWIN MORGAN
Department of English,
The University, Glasgow, W2.

Newmarket
This comes from *The Horseman's Word, A Sequence of Concrete Poems*, a *tour de force* of ten poems, all celebrating various aspects of the horse, and exemplifying Edwin Morgan's verbal resourcefulness to a peculiar degree. This poem should be spoken, *sotto voce*.

Aviemore Invernessshire August 1971
If you know D. H. Lawrence's poems on elephants in the circus (*The Complete Poems*, pp. 425–6), the last three lines of this poem will have added point.

Chicago May 1971

13   *The Fox* an anonymous hero of the environment movement in the States.
His strategy was to strike invisibly, wittily and pointedly.

Interferences
Edwin Morgan provided the following note on *Interferences* when they were
first published by the Midnight Press, Glasgow: I hope the general idea of
the poems is clear enough – it's the conception of 'other eyes watching' or
intersecting worlds or planes of existence, each spot of intersection/
interference being indicated by the spelling of a word suddenly going wrong.

Interferences 4
For other poems on Mary, Joseph and Jesus, see this volume, pages 48, 52,
and *Voices,* Book III, Penguin, pp. 60–65.

Interferences 5
The Marie Celeste was found drifting, with no one on board – all the crew
had disappeared without trace. The puzzle has never been satisfactorily
explained: until this poem was written.

ACKNOWLEDGEMENTS

The editor and publishers are very grateful to the following for permission to reproduce the poems in this anthology:

Charles Causley

For 'At the Grave of John Clare', 'I Saw a Shot-Down Angel', 'Ou Phrontis', 'Recruiting Drive', 'I Am the Great Sun', 'At the British War Cemetery, Bayeaux', 'Song of the Dying Gunner A.A.1', 'Chief Petty Officer' and 'Death of an Aircraft' from *Union Street*, published by Rupert Hart-Davis Ltd to the publishers and David Higham Associates Ltd. For 'Hymn for the Birth of a Royal Prince', 'By St Thomas Water', 'Reservoir Street', 'Dockacre', 'Death of a Poet', 'The Question', 'In Coventry' and 'Immunity' from *Underneath the Water*, published by Macmillan and Co. Ltd to the publishers and David Higham Associates Ltd. For 'Mary, Mary Magdalene' and 'The Reverend Sabine Baring-Gould' from *Figgie Hobbin*, published by Macmillan and Co. Ltd to the publishers and David Higham Associates Ltd. For 'Helpston' and 'Green Man in the Garden', published here for the first time, to the author and David Higham Associates Ltd.

Thom Gunn

For 'Tamer and Hawk' and 'Incident on a Journey' from *Fighting Terms*, published by Faber and Faber Ltd, to the author and the publishers. For 'On the Move' and 'The Unsettled Motorcyclist's Vision of his Death' from *The Sense of Movement*, published by Faber and Faber Ltd, to the author and the publishers. For 'Claus Von Stauffenberg' and 'Innocence' from *Selected Poems of Thom Gunn and Ted Hughes*, published by Faber and Faber Ltd, to the author and the publishers. For 'Flying Above California', 'Considering the Snail', 'Blackie, the Electric Rembrandt', 'My Sad Captains' and 'Epitaph for Anton Schmidt' from *Selected Poems 1950–66*, published by Faber and Faber Ltd, to the author and the publishers. For 'Taylor Street' and 'The Produce District' from *Touch*, published by Faber and Faber Ltd, to the author and the publishers. For 'Apartment Cats', 'Listening to Jefferson Airplane', 'The Discovery of the Pacific', 'Rites of Passage' and 'Street Song' from *Moly*, published by Faber and Faber Ltd, to the author and the publishers. For 'Second Take on *Rites of Passage*' by Robert Duncan to the author and the Poetry Society. For the poem 'Autobiography' to the author and the *Iowa Review*.

Seamus Heaney

For 'The Early Purges', 'Follower', 'The Diviner', 'Honeymoon Flight' and 'Digging' from *Death of a Naturalist*, published by Faber and Faber Ltd, to the author and the publishers. For 'Gone', 'The Salmon Fisher to the Salmon', 'The Forge', 'Rite of Spring' and 'Undine' from *Door into the Dark*, published by Faber and Faber Ltd, to the author and the publishers. For 'The Last Mummer', 'Toome', 'No Sanctuary', 'Midnight', 'The Tollund Man', 'Augury', 'Bye-Child', 'Westering' and 'The Dedicatory Poem' from *Wintering Out*, published by Faber and Faber Ltd, to the author and the publishers.

Ted Hughes

For 'The Thought-Fox', 'Song', 'The Jaguar', 'Wind', 'Griefs for Dead Soldiers' and 'Six Young Men' from *Hawk in the Rain*, published by Faber

280   *Acknowledgements*

and Faber Ltd, to the author and the publishers. For 'Crow Hill', 'A Dream of Horses', 'Esther's Tomcat', 'Relic', 'Witches', 'Thrushes', 'Pike' and 'Wilfred Owen's Photographs' from *Lupercal*, published by Faber and Faber Ltd, to the author and the publishers. For 'Second Glance at a Jaguar', 'Out', 'Heptonstall', 'Pibroch', 'Gnat-Psalm' and 'Full Moon and Little Frieda' from *Wodwo*, published by Faber and Faber Ltd, to the author and the publishers. For 'The Rock' from *Writers on Themselves*, published by BBC Publications, to the author and Olwyn Hughes. For a passage first published in the *Poetry Book Society Bulletin 15*, to the author and Olwyn Hughes.

Adrian Mitchell

For 'My Parents', 'Under Photographs of Two Party Leaders, Smiling', 'Open Day at Porton', 'Royal Poems', 'Final Chant', 'Solid Citizens' and 'Goodbye' from *Ride the Nightmare*, published by Jonathan Cape Ltd, to the author and the publishers. For 'Time and Motion Study', 'Veteran with a Head Wound', 'Early Shift on the *Evening Standard* News Desk' and 'Incident' from *Poems*, published by Jonathan Cape Ltd, to the author and the publishers. For 'Briefing', 'Norman Morrison', 'Hear the Voice of the Critic', 'Leaflets' and 'A Good Idea' from *Out Loud*, published by Jonathan Cape Ltd, to the author and the publishers. For 'Night Lines in a Peaceful Farmhouse', 'The Castaways *or* Vote for Caliban', 'Divide and Rule for as Long as You Can', 'Cease-Fire', 'The Marie Lloyd Song' and 'Bessie Smith in Yorkshire', published here for the first time, to the author.

Norman MacCaig

For a part of 'No End, No Beginning', 'Byre', 'Visiting Hour', 'Brooklyn Cop', 'Basking Shark' and 'Wild Oats' from *Selected Poems*, published by The Hogarth Press Ltd, to the author and the publishers. For 'Old Maps and New', 'Odd Man Out', 'Frustrated Virtuoso', 'Moon-Landing', 'New Tables' and 'Bookworm' from *White Bird*, published by The Hogarth Press Ltd, to the author and the publishers. For 'Aunt Julia' from *Rings on a Tree*, published by The Hogarth Press Ltd, to the author and the publishers. For 'Blind Horse', 'Boundaries', 'Beautiful Girl in a Gallery', 'Among the Talk and the Laughter', 'Television Studio', 'Changes in the Same Thing', 'Early Sunday Morning, Edinburgh', 'Incident', 'Nearing an End' and 'July Day Spectacular', published here for the first time, to the author.

Edwin Morgan

For 'Trio', 'Glasgow Green', 'The Suspect', 'In the Snack Bar', 'Message Clear', 'The Death of Marilyn Monroe', 'One Cigarette' and 'Spacepoem 3 : Off Course' from *A Second Life*, published by Edinburgh University Press, to the author and the publishers. For 'Two Glasgow Sonnets', 'For Bonfires', a passage from 'London', a passage from 'Interferences' and 'The First Men on Mercury' from *Glasgow to Saturn*, published by Carcanet Press, to the author and the publishers. For 'Glasgow 5 March 1971', 'Translunar Space March 1972', 'Bradford June 1972', 'Aviemore Invernessshire August 1971', 'Germany December 1970' and 'Chicago May 1971' from *Instamatic Poems*, published by Ian McKelvie, to the author and the publishers. For 'Newmarket' from *The Horseman's World*, published by Akros Publications, to the author and the publishers. For 'The Moon February 1973', published here for the first time, to the author.

INDEX OF FIRST LINES

INDEX OF TITLES